Busy People's Slow-Cooker Cookbook

Dawn Hall

Rutledge Hill Press™
Nashville, Tennessee
A Division of Thomas Nelson, Inc.
www.ThomasNelson.com

To one of my most favorite people in the world,
my mother, Wendy Ellen Oberhouse, whose
mouthwatering meals on more than one occasion
distracted me from the Sunday church service.

Published by Rutledge Hill Press, a Division of Thomas Nelson, Inc., P.O. Box 141000, Nashville, Tennessee, 37214.

Library of Congress Cataloging-in-Publication Data

Hall, Dawn.
Busy people's slow-cooker cookbook / by Dawn Hall.
    p. cm.
Includes index.
ISBN 1-4016-0107-3 (hidden spiral)
1. Electric cookery, Slow. 2. Quick and easy cookery. I. Title.
TX827.H35 2003
641.5'884—dc21
    2003001765

Printed in China
05 06 07 -10 9 8

Complete Your
Busy People's Library

The recipes in these two cookbooks are all easy to prepare
and cook They all contain 7 ingredients or less and can be
prepared in less than 30 minutes

**Down-Home Cooking
Without the Down-Home Fat**
1-4016-0104-9
$16.99

Includes recipes for:

- Citrus Pancakes
- Caesar Oyster Crackers
- Chicken Skillet Cobbler
- Chewy, Gooey No-Bake Freezer Cookies
- Turtle Cake

**Busy People's
Low-Fat Cookbook**
1-4016-0105-7
$16.99

Includes recipes for:

- Eight-layer Chili Casserole
- Steak and Potato Cattleman's Soup
- Cherry Oatmeal
- Peppermint Chocolate Cheesecake
- Butterfinger Trifle

Reviews from Real-Life Busy People

I wasn't expecting this to be such a great book. It is so full of great recipes! Usually you buy a recipe book and maybe try one or two but not with this book. This is a keeper. All the recipes are simple with only a few ingredients and almost no prep time. This was exactly what I needed to keep dinners sane in a very busy household with people eating at all different times.

I am a very busy mom and Dawn Hall's cookbooks have been a lifesaver for me. My family has loved everything I have fixed in the *Busy People's Slow Cooker Cookbook*. I can look up a recipe at the last minute and have all the ingredients 95% of the time. This is rare for me with other cookbooks.

As a working mother of two boys, this cookbook is a lifesaver! It is one of the better slow cooker cookbooks I've seen. The recipes are different than other ones I have seen, and they are all 7 ingredients or less. Gotta love that! It really does make life a lot easier. It is so nice to come home and have dinner ready and have it taste good. My husband and kids are always happy.

This cookbook has some of the best crock-pot recipes I've seen. Dawn Hall has outdone herself this time with a variety of delicious, easy to prepare dishes that all use 7 ingredients or less. You'll spend more time deciding which recipe to try first than actually making the meal!

Contents

Acknowledgments

T*hank you! Thank you! Thank you!*
   I am so blessed. God has surrounded me with a wonderful support team of people of integrity, character, and a high work ethic. Each of them is a vital part of this book's success.

It seems appropriate, since I thank God daily for these two very special people, that I first publicly acknowledge what a tremendous gift from God they both are to me. To my faithful, loyal, hardworking, and dedicated assistants, Karen Schwanbeck and Diane Bowman-Yantiss, I am and will always be grateful. You two are my right hand ladies. There's no way I could do all I do without you.

To Brenda Crosser, my test-cooking assistant, thank you for all of your help and helpful suggestions. I appreciate you.

To Jo Anna Lund, the unselfish, ever-giving, and caring author of *Healthy Exchanges Cookbooks,* thank you for your counsel and for introducing me to your literary agent. More importantly, thank you for being a living example of a godly, Christian businesswoman and author who truly runs her business and life by the Golden Rule.

To my literary agent, Coleen O'Shea, thank you for all you do on my behalf and for bringing Rutledge Hill Press and me together. We are a great fit.

To the staff at Rutledge Hill Press, I am grateful to be united with publishers of integrity such as you. I am blessed to be able to say my publishers don't publish anything I would be ashamed to be associated with. That means a lot to me.

Thank you, Tammi Hancock, a registered dietitian, for your expertise in getting accurate nutritional data for each recipe.

Last but not least, I want to thank my family. Often people think it would be wonderful to be at my dinner table every day eating something new or different I had created. But in all honesty, how would you like to be a guinea pig 365 days a year? They got tired of continually eating a meal prepared in the slow cooker—nonstop, day in and day out, until I finished this cookbook. For their patience and perseverance, I thank them.

My Story

It's been said that sometimes truth is stranger than fiction. Often this has been the case in my life. If I were not the one living my life, I'd find the truth of my life unbelievable. Many have said my story would make a great movie. Who knows? Maybe someday.

I was born in Fort Wayne, Indiana. My parents divorced when I was five. When I was ten we moved to Toledo, Ohio, when my mom remarried. I'm the oldest of seven. I feel I was born watching my weight and have struggled with being a compulsive overeater for as long as I can remember. I hate it.

I flunked first grade. In the early years of elementary school my teachers always told me I wasn't focusing in class, even though I was trying to with all my might. It wasn't until adulthood that I was diagnosed with attention deficit disorder, which explains my extreme difficulty (even today) concentrating with background noise and distractions. I graduated with honors in 1981 from Springfield High School.

I married my high school sweetheart, Tracy Wayne Hall, in 1984. I never went to college. I worked as a waitress until I was pregnant with our first child in 1986. We were blessed with two wonderful daughters born in 1987 and 1988. It took one year to physically build our small ranch home ourselves (with the help of friends) while our family lived in a tiny efficiency apartment above Tracy's parents' garage. We fondly named our new home Cozy Homestead, and we moved into it in June 1992.

I enjoyed teaching aerobics and facilitating classes for compulsive overeaters. With passion I was creating new recipes every day, and our family never ate the same meal twice for family dinners. I home-schooled our children until November 28, 1994. I'll never forget that day. It was the day my life was turned inside out and upside down and also the last day of a normal life as I can remember it.

November 28, 1994, the day after my loving husband's thirty-second birthday, was the day we found out Tracy had brain cancer. Doctors were able to surgically remove one pound of malignant tumor, leaving Tracy completely paralyzed on his entire left side. He was given six to eight months to live.

I told Tracy the day we found out about his cancer that I believed God was going to use our most challenging situation to give Himself praise and glory. That is *exactly* what God is doing to this day.

To make a long story short, in order to pay for an experimental treatment, we had to raise thousands of dollars each month because our insurance would not pay for experimental treatments. All of the recipes I had been creating over the previous five years I printed into books and sold in order to earn enough money for Tracy's treatments. My thought was we could use what little we had left in our savings to pay for a couple weeks of Tracy's treatment, or we could try to invest the money into cookbooks and hopefully earn enough to pay for his treatments indefinitely. In the beginning, when I was driving home with my first vanload of a thousand cookbooks I thought to myself, "You're nuts, Dawn. How in the world are you going to sell a thousand books? You're nuts!" Well, we sold a thousand cookbooks in five days and eighteen thousand cookbooks in ten weeks. That first book was *Down Home Cookin' without the Down Home Fat.* It was selected as one of Ohio's Best of the Best Cookbooks by Quail Ridge Press and the 1996 Best Cookbook of the Year by North American Book Dealers Exchange. Not too shabby for a homemaker who didn't know how to type or use a computer, huh? I would be a fool if I thought for even one moment that I did it. Over 650,000 cookbooks sold. It was definitely a God thing, and He gets all the credit. He did it through me and for that I am forever grateful.

I guess we weren't living with enough stress of daily financial bondage and fighting cancer and its devastating effects. We had a house fire on Valentine's Day in 2000. It was a nightmare, and I did all I could to fight the fire. I remember vividly our daughters screaming in panic and fear, "Get out of the house, Mom! It is only a house!" They were scared to death. All I knew was I didn't want our daughters to lose the house their daddy built for them. After all, how many little girls can say their daddy built their house for them? The fire left all four of us living in an assisted living nursing home for four months as builders restored our home back to its original state.

The good news was that Tracy lived for six and a half years after his diagnosis, twelve times longer than the doctors ever imagined. He was a wonderful father and an amazing example of a truly godly man. He inspired countless people, me included. He was able to fulfill his dream of living to see his little girls become young ladies. Tracy died on May 5, 2001. Ironically, it wasn't the cancer that took him. It was from a fall that caused a brain hemorrhage. The experimental treatment had cured him completely. Tracy's death was not in vain. The data gathered during his use of the experimental cancer treatment will be used to help others. All of his skin, bones, organs, and even part of his eyes were donated to help others live. Praise God!

God still gets all the praise and glory. I believe my cookbooks are a tool that God is using to open the doors for me to share the good news of His love. As an inspirational speaker, people will come listen to me, a "cookbook lady," when they might never come to listen to a preacher. I believe my primary purpose is to encourage and inspire others to live lives with no regrets and to put God first in their lives.

Introduction

Of all the cookbooks I have written, *Down Home Cookin' Without the Down Home Fat*, *Busy People's Low-Fat Cookbook*, and *Second Serving of Busy People's Low-Fat Recipes,* this book excites me the most because with a little bit of planning I am able to come home to a mouthwatering meal without having to wait at all to eat. I like that. I am confident without a doubt that you will also.

Whether you are a long-time user of slow cookers or this is your first time, I know you will enjoy this convenient and easy-to-use cookbook. Slow cookers are such time savers. Personally, I do not feel comfortable leaving home with my oven or stove on due to the risk of fire. However, cooking with a slow cooker is so safe that I don't think twice about leaving it cooking unattended all day long. Unlike conventional cooking, the slow cookers use less electricity than your refrigerator.

I really believe you are going to be thrilled at the many creative and unique ways to use a slow cooker. How would you like to cook absolutely gorgeous and exquisite cakes with luscious warm berries or sauces oozing down the sides of tall cakes that looked like they took all day to prepare? However, in all reality you prepared it with seven or fewer ingredients, and it took only minutes to assemble.

Easy to Use

Do you like the idea of putting together an entire meal fit for a king (or queen) in ten minutes or less and yet have it appear as if you have been slaving in the kitchen all day? To top it off, you can be gone the entire time the slow cooker is working. There is no need for constant attention or stirring. All you have to do is assemble the ingredients.

Are you thinking you are too busy to even assemble the handful of ingredients you need to use to prepare a mouthwatering meal before you leave for the day? Have no fear. Here's another great idea: Put the ingredients in the slow cooker the night before, and put the cooker in the refrigerator until the next morning. Then, in the morning, *voila!* Just take the cooker out of the refrigerator, plug it in, and turn it on before you leave. A scrumptious meal awaits you at home after a long day's work, and all you have to do when you get home is be ready to eat. Does good old-fashioned, home-style cooking get any easier or more delicious than this? Trust me, your family will be grateful. Mine is.

Savings

Another reason that I love slow cookers is the cost savings. You can use less expensive cuts of meat, and they always turn out absolutely tender, moist, and delicious. They are never dry or overcooked. Slow cookers cook slowly, and the moisture used when cooking with a slow cooker helps tenderize the meats. This is definitely a two-thumbs-up benefit for all of us.

Creative Uses

Using slow cookers in creative ways can also be a lifesaver. For example:

- Cooking in the dog days of a hot summer with a slow cooker is just the answer to helping keep the home cooler because slow cookers use a lot less energy than a conventional oven or stove.

Therefore a lot less heat is generated, leaving your kitchen a lot cooler than if you were cooking conventionally.

• I like to take my slow cooker camping, even tent camping. You may be wondering how in the world you take your slow cooker tent camping. It's simple. A lot of campgrounds have electrical outlets for tent campers. I just take along an extension cord and set the slow cooker on a hard surface inside our tent. If I go hiking, swimming, or cycling I make sure the tent is zipped up tight so no curious critters can get in and eat up our delicious meal or dessert awaiting us. This style of one-pot (slow cooker) cooking eliminates a lot of pots and pans to clean and leaves more time for fun and relaxation, and that is what camping is all about. Right? Sounds good to me. How about you?

Multiple Course Meals

Slow cookers are absolutely wonderful for multiple-course meals that would normally require multiple uses of the conventional oven. I love to serve desserts piping hot with either whipped cream or ice cream oozing down the sides. Doesn't your mouth begin watering just thinking of such a delight? Mine does. With slow cookers you can cook a fabulous dessert and serve it hot from the slow cooker immediately after dinner. There's no need to be preoccupied with the dessert details while you are preparing and cooking the entrée because you started the dessert hours before the dinner even began. No need to figure out how you are going to cook the entrée, the casserole, and the side dishes all in the oven at the same time at different temperatures and still have the dessert done without juggling a bunch of tasks. An added bonus is knowing your special dessert will be tasty and hot when you're ready to eat it. If the dessert is finished cooking before everyone is ready, don't worry. Simply unplug the slow cooker, and if it is possible, remove the crock insert. Your dessert will stay wonderfully warm until the perfect time for enjoying it.

Potlucks

Slow cookers are terrific for delivering meals as gifts to help out new moms, to someone who is sick, to a family going through a difficult time, or to new neighbors as a housewarming gift. You may even want to put a bow on the outside of the slow cooker along with a card stating the slow cooker is part of their housewarming gift. Don't keep the cooked food in the slow cooker too long since hot foods need to be kept at temperatures above 140 degrees in order to prevent the possibility of harmful bacteria growth.

I especially appreciate being able to take my slow cooker to potlucks or using it for buffets when I entertain large number of guests because I know my dish will be kept warm and tasty. If you are preparing a recipe from one of my cookbooks, you may want to save yourself time by writing the entire recipe on a note card and taping it to the outside of the slow cooker for others to copy. People are always requesting my recipes.

Low in Fat

Last, but certainly not least, another asset of this cookbook is that all of the recipes are low in fat. Many people out there think that if a recipe is low in fat it is low in flavor. This obviously could not be further from the truth, especially in my cookbooks. What most people care about when it comes to recipes is that they taste good and are fast and easy to make.

The recipes in this book are lower in fat because you won't be cooking with oil, even when you bake cakes. Also, I use cuts of meat that are lower in fat. If you substitute a fatty cut such a fat-marbled roast, make sure to cut off as much excess fat as possible before cooking. If you decide to substitute chicken with the skin on instead of boneless, skinless chicken, I encourage you to remove the skin, even if you decide to keep the bones in the chicken. An easy way to remove the skin from chicken that still has the bones is to remove the skin while the meat is still partially frozen, but not frozen solid.

If there is ever any excess fat floating on top of a soup or broth, you can easily remove it by skimming the fat off with a ladle, or lay a piece of thick paper towel on top of the soup or broth and let the grease be absorbed. Lift the fat-absorbed paper towel off and discard.

Slow-Cooker Sizes and Cooking Times

No matter how much of an extravagant cook you are, haven't we all had times when we just wanted a fast and easy meal as quickly as possible with as little effort as possible? In all honesty, aren't there times when we wanted that meal ten minutes ago? We've all been there at one time or another. These recipes give you what you want. All you have to do is invest ten to twenty minutes or less, and you can dash out the door looking forward to delicious dining when you get back. All it takes is a little thought beforehand. Preparing what you want to eat before you leave and coming home to a fully cooked meal sure beats coming home tired and hungry and then having to wait while you cook what you want to eat.

Slow cookers come in a variety of shapes and sizes. The most common size of slow cooker is the 3½-quart size. It will cook comfortably a four-pound chicken. Most of the recipes I cook are in the 3½-quart slow cooker, including all cakes and desserts. However, if you want to cook a side dish of a vegetable using a Pocket Pouch inside of the slow cooker while cooking the entrée, I encourage you to use the larger 6-quart slow cooker. It is better to have extra room in your slow cooker versus having all of your ingredients crammed into a smaller slow cooker. Remember, often the slow cooker creates more juices. Filling slow cookers too high can cause a mess, because the juices will overflow and run all over. Leave a good inch of space between the top of the edge of your slow cooker and the food. This gives the food plenty of room to breathe.

Cooking times vary depending on the temperature of the ingredients before cooking, how full the slow cooker is, and even the altitude. While creating and testing recipes, we have noticed that like conventional ovens, slow cookers themselves vary in temperature slightly. With this in mind, you will get to know your slow cooker, and you'll get to know what end of the time frame you will use for each recipe you prepare.

Unlike stovetop cooking, it is important you keep the lid on the slow cooker while cooking. Every time the lid is removed, up to 20 minutes of heat can escape. This means it may take up to an additional twenty minutes to cook your recipe.

If you have to remove the lid to add ingredients, then put it back on as quickly as possible. A perfect example of this is when we add pasta to some recipes 30 minutes or so before the end of cooking time.

Pocket Pouches

What Is a Pocket Pouch

Pocket pouches are my way of cooking an entire meal in the slow cooker without all of the ingredients blending together. A pocket pouch is a vegetable combination that can be cooked in the slow cooker on top of the entrée. Yes, one-dish meals such as soups, chowders, and casseroles are wonderful in their own right; however, there are times when we want our meat and vegetables prepared separately. These pocket pouches are just the answer.

I think you will be pleasantly surprised at the simplicity and diversity these pocket pouches give. You'll also like the flavorful combinations. You may be the creative type and find yourself creating your own unique and delicious pocket pouches.

How to Make a Pocket Pouch

Depending on the size of your slow cooker and how deep you want your pocket pouch to be, you will use approximately two strips of equal length heavy-duty aluminum foil measuring 18 to 24 inches.

On a counter top or flat surface lay the two strips of aluminum foil next to each other lengthwise and overlapping the foil one-half inch. Fold the overlapping pieces of foil over twice, forming a tightly sealed seam.

Press the foil with the shiny side facing outward into the slow cooker. This will form a bowl. Spray the inside of the foil bowl, or pocket pouch, with nonfat cooking spray. Place the vegetable combination of your choice into the pocket pouch along with seasonings. Fold the pocket pouch closed tightly. Place the lid on the slow cooker. Cook the entrée recipe as directed.

Please note: Depending on the temperature of the slow cooker, the temperature of vegetables being cooked, and the duration of cooking time, you may need to cook the entire meal up to a half hour longer, especially if the vegetables you are using are frozen. All of these pocket pouch vegetable combinations can be seasoned after cooking.

Pocket Pouch Vegetable Combinations

Asparagus: Put in 1 pound fresh asparagus and 1 ice cube and sprinkle with 1 tablespoon Butter Buds Sprinkles.

Broccoli & Beans: Put in 1 pound frozen broccoli (stems and pieces) and 1 pound frozen green beans. Sprinkle with 1 tablespoon Butter Buds Sprinkles.

Broccoli & Bacon: Put in 1 pound frozen broccoli (stems and pieces) and sprinkle with 1 tablespoon Butter Buds Sprinkles and 2 tablespoons real bacon bits.

California Blend: Put in a 1-pound bag California blend frozen vegetables (broccoli, cauliflower and carrots) and sprinkle with 1 tablespoon Butter Buds Sprinkles.

California Blend with Bacon: Put in a 1-pound bag California blend frozen vegetables (broccoli, cauliflower, and carrots) and sprinkle with 1 tablespoon Butter Buds Sprinkles and 2 tablespoons real bacon bits.

Carrots: Put in 1 pound fresh baby carrots and 1 ice cube and sprinkle with 1 tablespoon Butter Buds Sprinkles.

Glazed Carrots: Put in 1 pound fresh baby carrots, 1 ice cube, and 1 tablespoon honey.

Glazed Peas: Put in 1 pound frozen green peas and stir in 1 tablespoon of honey.

Glazed Peas and Onions: Put in 1 (10-ounce) box frozen peas and onion combination and stir in 1 tablespoon honey.

Green Beans: Put in 1 pound frozen green beans and sprinkle with 1 tablespoon Butter Buds Sprinkles.

Green Beans with Bacon: Put in 1 pound frozen green beans and sprinkle with 1 tablespoon Butter Buds Sprinkles and 1 tablespoons real bacon bits.

Green Beans with Ham: Put in 1 pound frozen green beans and ¼ pound chopped lean ham and sprinkle with 1 tablespoon Butter Buds Sprinkles.

Green Beans with Mushrooms & Onions: Put in 1 pound frozen green beans, 1 (4-ounce) can sliced mushrooms (or 4 ounces fresh sliced mushrooms), half of a small onion sliced into thin strips, and 1 ice cube and sprinkle with 1 tablespoon Butter Buds Sprinkles.

Green Beans with Onions: Put in 1 pound frozen green beans and 1 small onion sliced into thin strips and sprinkle with 1 tablespoon Butter Buds Sprinkles.

Italian Blend Vegetables: Put in 1 pound Italian blend frozen vegetables and sprinkle with 1 tablespoon Butter Buds Sprinkles.

Italian Blend Vegetables with Bacon: Put in 1 pound Italian blend frozen vegetables and 2 tablespoons of bacon bits and sprinkle with 1 tablespoon Butter Buds Sprinkles.

Mushrooms: Put in 1 pound fresh mushrooms (either sliced or whole) and 1 ice cube and sprinkle with 1 tablespoon Butter Buds Sprinkles.

Mushrooms & Onions: Put in ½ pound fresh mushrooms (either sliced or whole). Add 1 medium onion sliced thinly and 1 ice cube and sprinkle with 1 tablespoon Butter Buds Sprinkles.

Oriental Blend: Put in 1 pound bag frozen oriental vegetables and sprinkle with 1 tablespoon Butter Buds Sprinkles.

Peas: Put in 1 pound frozen peas and sprinkle with 1 tablespoon Butter Buds Sprinkles.

Pea Pods: Put in 1 pound fresh pea pods and 1 ice cube and sprinkle with 1 tablespoon Butter Buds Sprinkles.

Pepper Blend: Cut into ¼-inch slices 1 each fresh green pepper, fresh yellow pepper, and fresh red pepper. Add 1 ice cube and sprinkle with 1 tablespoon Butter Buds Sprinkles.

Spiced Apples: Put in 4 cored and sliced Jonathan apples with 2 tablespoons Butter Buds Sprinkles, 1 teaspoon ground cinnamon, ¼ cup dark brown sugar, and 2 tablespoons water.

Spinach: Put in 2 (10-ounce) boxes frozen spinach and sprinkle with 1 tablespoon Butter Buds Sprinkles.

Spinach with Bacon: Put in 2 (10-ounce) boxes frozen spinach and sprinkle with 1 tablespoon Butter Buds Sprinkles and 2 tablespoons real bacon bits.

Spinach with Ham: Put in 2 (10-ounce) boxes of frozen spinach and sprinkle with 1 tablespoon Butter Buds Sprinkles. Then stir in 4 ounces extra lean ham cut into tiny pieces. (The meat section often has finely chopped ham prepackaged.)

Waxed Beans: Put in 1 pound fresh waxed green beans and 1 ice cube and sprinkle with 1 tablespoon Butter Buds Sprinkles.

Waxed Beans with Bacon: Put in 1 pound of fresh waxed green beans and 1 ice cube and sprinkle with 1 tablespoon Butter Buds Sprinkles and 2 tablespoons real bacon bits.

Waxed Beans with Ham: Put in 1 pound fresh waxed green beans and 4 ounces extra lean ham cut into tiny pieces and sprinkle with 1 tablespoon Butter Buds Sprinkles.

Zucchini Strips: Put in 1 pound thinly sliced zucchini and 1 ice cube and sprinkle with 1 tablespoon Butter Buds Sprinkles.

Butter Buds

I use Butter Buds in a lot of my recipes. Butter Buds is a brand name product. It is all natural, fat- and cholesterol-free butter-flavored granules that can be used in place of butter, margarine, or oil. It is available in granulated Sprinkles and a Mix, which can be reconstituted with hot water to form a buttery liquid. Both forms may also be substituted for butter, margarine or oil as an ingredient in low-fat cooking and baking. Because they are low in fat and can be used in baking, I have depended on them for a number of my recipes. The

BUTTER BUDS® SUBSTITUTION CHART

Butter or Margarine	Butter Buds Mix (Dry)	Butter Buds Mix (Liquified)	Butter Buds Sprinkles
1 tablespoon	1 teaspoon	1 tablespoon	¾ teaspoon
2 tablespoons	2 teaspoons	2 tablespoons	1½ teaspoons
¼ cup (½ stick)	4 teaspoons (½ envelope)	¼ cup	1 tablespoon
½ cup (1 stick)	8 teaspoons (1 envelope)	½ cup	2 tablespoons
1 cup (2 sticks)	2 envelopes	1 cup	¼ cup

Butter Buds® is a registered trademark of Cumberland Packaging Corp., Brooklyn, New York, 11205. Used by Permission.

chart above shows substitutions in case you cannot find Butter Buds at your local grocer.

Mueller's Brand Pasta

For the pasta recipes in this book it is important to use Muellers brand pasta. It is the only brand (except no-yolk noodles) that I have found to hold up during these lengthy cooking times. If your local grocer doesn't carry Muellers pasta, you can order it from www.premiumproductsllc.com or call toll free 1-866-283-1400.

Breakfast

Swallow your pride—it's not fattening. . . . Actually, it's good for you!

Banana Cream Oatmeal

If you like Banana Cream Pie, you'll love this.

4 cups water	2 cups old-fashioned oats, dry
1/2 cup fat-free, sweetened condensed skim milk	2 medium bananas, thinly sliced into 1/4-inch pieces

- Spray a slow cooker with nonfat cooking spray.
- Place the water, condensed milk, and oats in the slow cooker.
- Cover and cook on low for 6 hours. (Add the bananas 5 minutes before serving.)
- Serve warm.

Yield: 4 (1½-cup) servings

Calories: 312; Fat: 3g (9% fat); Cholesterol: 2mg; Carbohydrate: 65g; Dietary Fiber: 5g; Protein: 9g; Sodium: 42mg

 Menu idea: This is best served with skim milk, tea, or coffee.

Cherry Oatmeal

The slight tartness of the cherries is a pleasant fruity surprise. Children especially like this fruity oatmeal.

6 cups water	1 (21-ounce) can light cherry pie filling
1/4 teaspoon salt, optional	3/4 cup strawberry-flavored powdered sugar*
3 cups old-fashioned oats, dry	
1 teaspoon almond extract	

- Spray a slow cooker with nonfat cooking spray.
- Mix the water, salt, oats, almond extract, pie filling, and powdered sugar together in the slow cooker.
- Cover and cook on low for 6 hours.
- Serve warm.

*Note: If you don't have strawberry-flavored powdered sugar, regular powdered sugar will be fine.

Yield: 7 (1-cup) servings

Calories: 215; Fat: 3g (10% fat); Cholesterol: 0mg; Carbohydrate: 44g; Dietary Fiber: 4g; Protein: 5g; Sodium: 11mg

 Menu idea: This is a great treat for breakfast with toast and milk.

Coconut Cream Oatmeal

Smooth, creamy, and satisfying.

2	tablespoons coconut flakes	1/2	cup fat-free, sweetened condensed skim milk
1/4	teaspoon light salt, optional		
4	cups water	1	teaspoon coconut extract
2	cups old-fashioned oats, dry		

- Spray a slow cooker with nonfat cooking spray.
- Mix the coconut, salt, water, oats, condensed milk, and coconut extract together in the slow cooker.
- Cover and cook on low for 6 hours.
- Serve warm.

Yield: 4 (1-cup) servings

Calories: 272; Fat: 4g (12% fat); Cholesterol: 2mg; Carbohydrate: 53g; Dietary Fiber: 4g; Protein: 9g; Sodium: 47mg

 Menu idea: This breakfast treat is very good with a little pineapple added.

Cran-Apple Oatmeal

This will wake up your taste buds. It is very good.

2¹/₂ cups apple cider
1¹/₂ cups old-fashioned oats, dry

¹/₃ cup sweetened dried
cranberries

- Spray a slow cooker with nonfat cooking spray.
- In the slow cooker mix together the apple cider, oats, and cranberries.
- Cover and cook on low for 6 hours.
- Serve warm.

Yield: 3 (1-cup) servings

Calories: 285; Fat: 3g (10% fat); Cholesterol: 0mg; Carbohydrate: 61g; Dietary
Fiber: 5g; Protein: 6g; Sodium: 22mg

 Menu idea: This is a great breakfast served with skim milk or tea.

Blueberry Coffee Cake

You may be wondering, "Why cook it in the slow cooker?" The answer is that while your conventional oven is already baking something else at a different temperature, this tasty coffee cake can also be cooking.

1 (6½-ounce) blueberry muffin mix, dry—Do not make as directed on package.	1 egg white
	⅛ teaspoon ground cinnamon
¼ cup fat-free skim milk	

- Preheat a slow cooker by turning it on high. Let it preheat for 10 minutes.
- Spray the cooker with nonfat cooking spray and cover.
- Set aside ¼ cup of the dry muffin mix. (Reserve for later.)
- In a medium–size bowl stir together the muffin mix (do not use the ¼ cup muffin mix reserved for later), milk, and egg white until well mixed. The batter will be lumpy. Spread it into the prepared cooker.
- Stir together the ¼ cup reserved dry muffin mix with the cinnamon until well mixed. Sprinkle the mixture on top of the batter in the slow cooker.
- Place a paper towel over the slow cooker and cover with the lid. Cook on high for 1 hour.
- Let the cake cool for 10 minutes. Run a knife along the edge of the cake to loosen it. Place a plate on top of the cooker and turn it upside down to remove the cake. Put another plate on top of the upside down cake and flip the cake right side up.
- Cut into 6 pie-shaped pieces.

Yield: 6 servings

Calories: 115; Fat: 3g (24% fat); Cholesterol: 5mg; Carbohydrate: 19g; Dietary Fiber: 0g; Protein: 2g; Sodium: 150mg

 Menu idea: I like to serve this for breakfast or brunch buffets. It is also great as a snack or for packed lunches.

Fruit Cocktail Coffee Cake

I surprised myself with how light and delicious this is. It is also very pretty with the layers of oats visible. I used a small, 3-quart slow cooker.

6 egg whites	in the mix, dry—Do not make as directed on box.
1 (15-ounce) can light fruit cocktail, drain and keep juice	1/2 plus 1/2 cup quick-cooking oats
1 (18 1/2-ounce) super moist yellow cake mix with pudding	1/2 plus 1/2 teaspoon cinnamon

- Preheat a slow cooker on high for 10 minutes.
- Spray the cooker with nonfat cooking spray.
- With a mixer beat the egg whites and the juice from the fruit cocktail in a medium-size bowl for 30 seconds.
- Add the cake mix and beat for 2 minutes longer.
- Pour half the cake batter into the prepared slow cooker.
- Arrange half the can of fruit cocktail on top of the batter.
- Sprinkle 1/2 cup oats over the fruit cocktail. Sprinkle 1/2 teaspoon cinnamon over the oats. Pour the remaining cake batter over the fruit and oats.
- Arrange the remaining half can fruit cocktail on top and sprinkle the remaining oats over the fruit and the remaining cinnamon over the oats.
- Place a paper towel on top of the slow cooker and cover with the lid.
- Cook on high for 2 hours.
- Take the ceramic crock out of the slow cooker. Take off the lid and the paper towel. Let the cake cool for 10 minutes. Run a knife around the edge of the cake to loosen it from the crock.
- Place a large dinner plate on top of the slow cooker and turn it over to remove the cake. Place another large dinner plate on top of the upside down cake and turn both plates (with the cake in the middle) over again so the cake will be right side up.
- Refrigerate any leftover cake.

Yield: 12 servings

Calories: 232; Fat: 4g (15% fat); Cholesterol: 0mg; Carbohydrate: 45g; Dietary Fiber: 1g; Protein: 5g; Sodium: 323mg

 Menu idea: This is delicious served warm with a dab of fat-free whipped topping or served chilled.

Cappuccino Cake

Oh, so good!

I (18.25-ounce) devil's food, super moist cake mix, dry (I use Betty Crocker.) Do not make as directed on box.	4 egg whites
	I tablespoon instant coffee
	I teaspoon ground cinnamon
1¹/₃ cups water	¹/₂ cup applesauce

- Preheat a 5-quart slow cooker for 10 minutes on high.
- Spray the ceramic insert with nonfat cooking spray.
- In a medium-size bowl beat the cake mix, water, egg whites, instant coffee, cinnamon, and applesauce on low speed for 1 minute, scraping the bowl constantly. (Or stir by hand for 2 minutes.)
- Pour the mixture into the prepared slow cooker, put a paper towel over the top, and cover with the lid.
- Cook for 2 hours on high or until a knife inserted in the center comes out clean.
- Let the cake cool for 10 minutes.
- Turn the slow cooker upside down to remove the cake.

Yield: 12 servings

Calories: 192; Fat: 4g (19% fat); Cholesterol: 0mg; Carbohydrate: 35g; Dietary Fiber: 1g; Protein: 3g; Sodium: 350mg

 Menu idea: This cake is great served with frozen yogurt.

Sunrise Soufflé

Serving this soufflé while the sun comes up will make even the prettiest of sunrises more enjoyable.

6 slices fat-free bread, cubed	2 cups skim milk
1 (8-ounce) package breakfast sausage links, sliced (I use Morningstar Farms.)	1 teaspoon dry mustard
1½ cups Egg Beaters	1 cup shredded low-fat cheddar cheese

- Spray a slow cooker with nonfat cooking spray.
- Add the bread cubes and sausage slices.
- In a bowl mix the eggs, milk, and dry mustard.
- Pour the mixture over the bread and sausage (already in slow cooker).
- Sprinkle the cheese on top.
- Cover and cook on low for 3 to 4 hours.

Note: This can be varied by adding lean ham or bacon bits.

Yield: 12 servings

Calories: 109; Fat: 1g (7% fat); Cholesterol: 3mg; Carbohydrate: 12g; Dietary Fiber: 1g; Protein: 13g; Sodium: 372mg

 Menu idea: This is great with Mini-Cinnamon Rolls from *Busy People's Low-Fat Cookbook.*

Appetizers

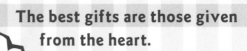

The best gifts are those given from the heart.

Mint Tea

There's no need to purchase those expensive small bottles of mint tea anymore.

2	quarts hot water	8	tea bags
	Splenda	2	drops mint extract

- Put the water and Splenda to taste in a slow cooker and mix until the sugar is dissolved.
- Add the tea bags and mint extract.
- Cover and cook on high for 2 hours.

Yield: 8 (1-cup) servings

Calories: 2; Fat: 0g (0% fat); Cholesterol: 0mg; Carbohydrate: 1g; Dietary Fiber: 0g; Protein: 0g; Sodium: 7mg

 Menu idea: I like to serve this hot for breakfast buffets, and I like to keep a pitcher of it in the refrigerator to serve chilled.

Spiced Tea

The aroma when preparing this tea makes the entire house smell good.

1	gallon hot water	1/2	cup brown sugar
8	tea bags	2	teaspoons ground cinnamon
2	tablespoons cinnamon candies (I use Red Hots.)	1/2	teaspoon ground allspice

- In a large slow cooker mix together the water, tea bags, candies, brown sugar, cinnamon, and allspice. Stir until the seasonings are dissolved.
- Cover and cook on low for 8 hours.
- Remove the tea bags. Ready to drink as is, or served over ice.

Yield: 16 (1-cup) servings

Calories: 35; Fat: 0g (0% fat); Cholesterol: 0mg; Carbohydrate: 9g;
Dietary Fiber: 0g; Protein: 0g; Sodium: 6mg

 Menu idea: If you cook this overnight, it makes a great breakfast drink instead of coffee.

Honey Mustard Piggy Dippers

Appetizers can't get much easier than this, folks.

I (14-ounce) package fat-free smoked sausage	¹/₂ cup fat-free honey mustard salad dressing (I use Marzetti's.)

- Spray a slow cooker with nonfat cooking spray.
- Cut the sausage into ¹/₂-inch chunks.
- Put the sausage and salad dressing in the slow cooker and stir, making sure all the sausage is coated.
- Cover and cook on low for 3 hours.
- Serve with toothpicks.

Note: For parties make a double batch and keep it in the slow cooker.

Yield: 7 (2-ounce) appetizer servings

Calories: 87; Fat: 0g (0% fat); Cholesterol: 24mg; Carbohydrate: 13g;
Dietary Fiber: 0g; Protein: 9g; Sodium: 830mg

Yield: 4 (3¹/₂-ounce) entrée servings

Calories: 153; Fat: 0g (0% fat); Cholesterol: 43mg; Carbohydrate: 22g;
Dietary Fiber: 0g; Protein: 15g; Sodium: 1453mg

 Menu idea: These are great for parties and large gatherings.

Chili Cheeser Pleaser Dip

This thick, hearty dip is a favorite with men.

I	pound eye of round beef, ground	8	ounces fat-free fancy shredded cheddar cheese (I use Kraft.)
2	(15-ounce) cans fat-free chili with black beans (I use Health Valley spicy vegetarian.)	I	(4-ounce) can diced green chiles

- Spray a slow cooker with nonfat cooking spray.
- In the slow cooker mix together the eye of round, chili, cheese, and chiles.
- Cover and cook on high for 3 hours.

Yield: 15 (3½-ounce) servings

Calories: 129; Fat: 3g (22% fat); Cholesterol: 13mg; Carbohydrate: 8g; Dietary Fiber: 3g; Protein: 14g; Sodium: 216mg

 Menu idea: You may want to spread this dip out on a large plate after cooking and top it with salsa. Serve with baked tortilla chips.

Sweet and Sour Teenie-Weenies

Children especially think these are fun to eat.

1 (14-ounce) package fat-free hot dogs	1/4 cup grape jelly
	2 tablespoons mustard

- Slice each hot dog diagonally into 5 pieces.
- In a medium slow cooker mix the jelly and mustard together until well mixed.
- Add the hot dogs and coat with the sauce.
- Cover and cook on low for 3 hours.
- Serve with toothpicks.

Note: This recipe can be tripled and kept warm on low in a slow cooker for up to 4 hours.

Yield: 16 (½-hot dog) servings

Calories: 31; Fat: 0g (0% fat); Cholesterol: 7mg; Carbohydrate: 5g; Dietary Fiber: 0g; Protein: 3g; Sodium: 267mg

 Menu idea: These are great as an appetizer or as hors d'oeuvres. They serve well at picnics and potlucks.

Mexican Confetti Dip

Share with friends; they'll love it.

1 (12-ounce) can whole kernel corn, drained	1/3 cup fat-free Italian salad dressing (I use Marzetti.)
1 (15 1/2-ounce) can black beans, drained	1 (16-ounce) jar chunky salsa

- Spray a slow cooker with nonfat cooking spray.
- In the slow cooker mix together the corn, black beans, salad dressing, and salsa.
- Cover and cook on low for 4 hours.
- Serve with baked tortilla chips.

Yield: 11 (1/2-cup) servings

Calories: 71; Fat: 1g (9% fat); Cholesterol: 0mg; Carbohydrate: 10g; Dietary Fiber: 3g; Protein: 3g; Sodium: 490mg

 Menu idea: Warm a flour tortilla in the microwave. Fill the center with 1/4 cup of the dip. Fold up as you would a burrito. Toss 1/2 cup of the dip with 1 1/2 cups of your favorite lettuces for a tasty twist to your salad.

V. J.'s Bean Dip

This recipe was given to me by Vicky Graf. I changed it to low-fat, and it's still very good.

1 (12-ounce) bag ground meatless burger (I use Morningstar Farms.)	1 (14-ounce) can refried beans
	8 ounces Velveeta Lite, cubed (if you like it spicy use Mexican Velveeta Lite)
1 medium onion, chopped	
1 green pepper, chopped	1 cup salsa, your favorite

- Spray a slow cooker with nonfat cooking spray.
- In the slow cooker mix together the meatless burger, onion, pepper, refried beans, cheese, and salsa.
- Cover and cook on low for 8 hours or on high for 4 hours.
- Serve with baked tortilla chips.

Note: To make a Mexican salad using the bean dip, spray the bottom of a microwave cereal bowl with nonstick spray. Mold a fat-free tortilla over the bowl and cook on high for 2 minutes or until crisp. Use for the salad.

Yield: 8 (½-cup) servings

Calories: 177; Fat: 3g (16% fat); Cholesterol: 12mg; Carbohydrate: 18g; Dietary Fiber: 5g; Protein: 17g; Sodium: 932mg

 Menu idea: Fill the tortilla bowl with chopped lettuce, tomatoes, chopped onion, and Bean Dip. Top with fat-free sour cream, fat-free shredded cheddar cheese, and salsa.

Warm Watchamacallit

This is great during the autumn cool days and nights.

2	quarts cider	1/2	cup red cinnamon candies
1	liter diet ginger ale		Cinnamon sticks, optional

- In a slow cooker mix together the cider, ginger ale, and cinnamon candies.
- Cover and cook on high for 4 hours.
- Serve warm with a cinnamon stick.

Yield: 12 (1-cup) servings

Calories: 118; Fat: 0g (0% fat); Cholesterol: 0mg; Carbohydrate: 29g; Dietary Fiber: 0g; Protein: 0g; Sodium: 29mg

 Menu idea: This recipe complements cookies, such as Spice Cookies from *Busy People's Low-Fat Cookbook.*

Breads

It doesn't take funds to have fun.

Cottage Cheese Bread

I love using my slow cooker for wonderful breads like this. It is so convenient.

1 cup fat-free cottage cheese	$^3/_4$ cup skim milk
4 ounces Egg Beaters (or 4 egg whites)	1 teaspoon vanilla
	$2^3/_4$ cups reduced-fat baking mix
1 cup sugar	$^1/_2$ cup raisins or dried cranberries

- Preheat a slow cooker on high while you prepare the recipe (at least 10 minutes).
- Spray the slow cooker with nonfat cooking spray.
- In a bowl mix together the cottage cheese, Egg Beaters, sugar, milk, vanilla, baking mix, and cranberries.
- Pour the mixture in the slow cooker, cover, and cook on high for 2 hours.

Yield: 8 servings

Calories: 320; Fat: 3g (8% fat); Cholesterol: 3mg; Carbohydrate: 65g; Dietary Fiber: 1g; Protein: 9g; Sodium: 616mg

 Menu idea: You can decorate the top of the bread with chopped cherries and sprinkle with sugar before cooking if desired.

Fiesta Bread

Quickly mixed together in a zip, and it has a zippy flavor, too.

2 cups reduced-fat baking mix (I use Bisquick.)	4½ teaspoons taco seasoning mix
⅔ cup skim milk	Buttered-flavored nonstick spray

- Preheat a slow cooker while you prepare the recipe.
- Spray the slow cooker with nonfat cooking spray. In a bowl mix well the baking mix, skim milk, and taco seasoning mix.
- Pour the batter into the slow cooker and pat down.
- Spray the top with the nonstick spray.
- Cover and cook on high for 1 hour.

Yield: 8 servings

Calories: 126; Fat: 2g (14% fat); Cholesterol: 0mg; Carbohydrate: 24g; Dietary Fiber: 0g; Protein: 3g; Sodium: 514mg

 Menu idea: For a different variation, substitute dry onion soup mix for the taco seasoning.

Grandma Schaefer's Apple Butter

This is my absolutely, positively, number-one-favorite apple butter recipe.

10 cups cooked apples (about 12 large apples, cored) cooked in about ¼ cup water	1 teaspoon cinnamon
	1 teaspoon allspice
	½ teaspoon ground cloves
6 cups sugar	Paraffin, optional

- Put the cooked apples in a blender. Blend until all the apples are ground up. Put the ground apples into a slow cooker.
- Add the sugar, cinnamon, allspice, and cloves.
- Cover and cook in a slow cooker on low for 17 hours. Stir once in a while. Take the lid off for the last 2 hours.
- Fill a canning jar ½-inch shy of the top. Melt the paraffin and pour over. If you don't want to can it, just keep it refrigerated.

Yield: 256 (1-tablespoon) servings

Calories: 24; Fat: 0g (0% fat); Cholesterol: 0mg; Carbohydrate: 6g; Dietary Fiber: 0g; Protein: 0g; Sodium: 0mg

 Menu idea: This spread is great on toast, bagels, or bread. It is wonderful over fat-free frozen yogurt or fat-free ice cream, or even on slices of angel food cake. I love to eat this with fat-free cottage cheese.

Parmesan Garlic Quick Bread

Who would have ever thought bread cooked in a slow cooker could taste so good?

1½ cups reduced-fat baking mix	1 tablespoon sugar
2 egg whites	1 tablespoon garlic powder
½ cup skim milk	¼ cup reduced-fat Parmesan cheese
1 tablespoon dried minced onion	

- Preheat a slow cooker on high as you prepare the recipe.
- In a medium-size bowl stir together the baking mix, egg whites, milk, onion, sugar, and garlic powder and mix well.
- Spray the slow cooker with nonfat cooking spray and pour in the bread mixture.
- Sprinkle with the Parmesan cheese.
- Cover and cook on high for 1 hour.

Note: For leftover bread, slice, spray with Pam, and toast on the grill. Really good.

Yield: 8 servings

Calories: 121; Fat: 2g (17% fat); Cholesterol: 3mg; Carbohydrate: 21g; Dietary Fiber: 0g; Protein: 4g; Sodium: 340mg

 Menu idea: This bread is great with hot soup, Italian dishes, or salads.

Peachy Pumpkin Bread

Every once in a while when I'm trying to create a new recipe, I'm pleasantly surprised by how great it turns out. This is one of those recipes. It's even better than I thought it'd be.

1 (29-ounce) can sliced peaches, drained and cut into tiny pieces	1 (14-ounce) box quick pumpkin bread mix, dry (I use Pillsbury.) Do not make as directed on box.
1 egg	1 cup quick-cooking oats
2 egg whites	1 cup water

- Preheat a slow cooker to high for 10 minutes.
- Spray the slow cooker with nonfat cooking spray.
- With a mixer beat the peaches, egg, egg whites, pumpkin bread mix, oats, and water together for 1½ to 2 minutes or until well mixed.
- Pour the mixture into the prepared slow cooker.
- Lay a paper towel on the top of the slow cooker. Put the lid on the top of the paper towel to cover.
- Cover and cook on high for 2 hours.
- Take the ceramic crock out of the slow cooker. Take off the lid and remove the paper towel. Let the bread cool for 10 minutes.
- Run a knife around the edge of the bread to loosen it from the crock.
- Place a large dinner plate on top of the slow cooker and turn it over to remove the bread. Place another large dinner plate on top of the upside down bread. Turn both plates (with the bread in the middle) over again so the bread will be facing right side up.
- Keep any unused portions refrigerated.

Yield: 12 servings

Calories: 189; Fat: 2g (11% fat); Cholesterol: 18mg; Carbohydrate: 37g; Dietary Fiber: 2g; Protein: 5g; Sodium: 207mg

 Menu idea: This is great for breakfast, snacks, or brunch.

Southwestern Corn Bread

A tasty twist to an old-time favorite.

¹/₃ cup plus 1 tablespoon chunky salsa	2 egg whites
2 tablespoons cinnamon-flavored applesauce	1 (8¹/₂-ounce) box corn bread mix

- Spray a slow cooker with nonfat cooking spray.
- In a bowl combine the salsa, applesauce, and egg whites and mix well.
- Add the corn bread mix. Stir until well mixed. (Batter will be lumpy.)
- Pour into the prepared slow cooker.
- Cover and cook on high for 1¹/₂ hours or on low for 3 hours.

Yield: 8 servings

Calories: 136; Fat: 4g (25% fat); Cholesterol: 1mg; Carbohydrate: 22g; Dietary Fiber: 2g; Protein: 3g; Sodium: 404mg

 Menu idea: This bread is great with the Southwestern Vegetarian Soup (page 59), bean-based soups, and chowders.

Sweet Corn Bread

Who would ever think corn bread that tastes this good could be cooked in a slow cooker?

1/3 cup Egg Beaters	1 teaspoon salt, optional
1 cup evaporated skim milk	1 1/4 cup reduced-fat baking mix
1/2 cup brown sugar	(I use Bisquick.)
2 teaspoons dry butter substitute (I use Molly McButter.)	3/4 cup cornmeal

- Spray a slow cooker with nonfat cooking spray and preheat for 10 minutes.
- In a large bowl combine the Egg Beaters, milk, and sugar.
- Add the butter substitute and salt, if using. Mix thoroughly.
- Add the baking mix and cornmeal and stir until well mixed.
- Pour the mixture into the slow cooker.
- Cover and cook for 1 hour on high. (Do not cook on low.)

Yield: 9 servings

Calories: 179; Fat: 1g (7% fat); Cholesterol: 1mg; Carbohydrate: 36g; Dietary Fiber: 1g; Protein: 5g; Sodium: 267mg

 Menu idea: Great served with bean-based soups, chowders, ham, and lean pork.

Soups & Salads

A casual friend brings a gift to your party. A true friend comes early to help you cook and stays late to help you clean.

Beef & Potato Soup

People who are "meat and potato" eaters especially tend to like this soup.

4 cups water	2 (4-ounce) cans mushroom stems and pieces, not drained
I (16-ounce) bag frozen, Southern style hash browns	I (1-ounce) envelope dry onion soup mix
I cup frozen chopped onion or I medium onion, chopped	I (16-ounce) jar chunky salsa
I pound ground eye of round beef, cut into bite-size pieces	

- Spray a slow cooker with nonfat cooking spray.
- Put into the slow cooker the water, hash browns, onion, beef, mushrooms, onion soup mix, and salsa and stir until well mixed.
- Cover and cook in the slow cooker on high for 4 hours or on low for 8 to 9 hours.
- If desired, salt and pepper to taste.

Yield: 11 (1-cup) servings

Calories: 137; Fat: 4g (27% fat); Cholesterol: 15mg; Carbohydrate: 13g; Dietary Fiber: 2g; Protein: 10g; Sodium: 629mg

 Menu idea: The Crunchy Cucumbers with Cream from *Busy People's Low-Fat Cookbook* and the Sweet Corn Bread on page 41 of this book make this a complete meal.

Beef Barley Soup

This comfort soup satisfies the soul.

1 (48-ounce) can fat-free beef broth	1 cup frozen chopped onion
1 (28-ounce) can crushed tomatoes	2 cups frozen sliced carrots
1½ pounds lean, cooked steak, cut into bite-size pieces (Grilled eye of round is a good choice.)	1 cup chopped celery
	½ cup quick-cooking barley, not cooked

- Spray a slow cooker with nonfat cooking spray.
- In the slow cooker mix together the broth, tomatoes, steak, onion, carrots, and celery.
- Cover and cook on high for 5 hours or on low for 8 to 10 hours.
- Stir in the barley.
- Cover and cook for an additional 10 to 12 minutes or until the barley is tender.

Note: This is a great way to use leftover beef. I especially like using steak that's been cooked on the grill.

Yield: 11 (1-cup) servings

Calories: 173; Fat: 3g (17% fat); Cholesterol: 43mg; Carbohydrate: 13g; Dietary Fiber: 3g; Protein: 22g; Sodium: 703mg

 **Menu idea:** Serve this with Crunchy Cucumbers with Cream from *Busy People's Low-Fat Cookbook.*

Beef Noodle Soup

This flavorful soup is one everyone thinks is great.

1	(48-ounce) can fat-free beef broth	1	cup frozen chopped onion
1	(28-ounce) can crushed tomatoes	2	cups frozen sliced carrots
1 1/2	pounds cooked steak, cut into bite-size pieces (Grilled eye of round beef is a good choice.)	1	cup chopped celery
		2	cups uncooked egg noodles

- Spray a slow cooker with nonfat cooking spray.
- In the slow cooker combine the broth, tomatoes, steak, onion, carrots, and celery.
- Cover and cook on high for 5 hours or on low for 8 to 10 hours.
- Turn the slow cooker to high (if previously cooking on low) 10 minutes before adding the noodles.
- Stir in the noodles.
- Cover and cook for an additional 10 to 15 minutes or until the noodles are tender. Do not overcook.

Note: You can substitute 1 1/2 pounds ground eye of round that has been browned in a skillet and drained.

Yield: 12 (1-cup) servings

Calories: 162; Fat: 3g (18% fat); Cholesterol: 45mg; Carbohydrate: 12g; Dietary Fiber: 2g; Protein: 21g; Sodium: 646mg

 Menu idea: My mother-in-law likes to serve this over mashed potatoes. For a super easy recipe, use my Mashed Potatoes Deluxe from *Busy People's Low-Fat Cookbook*. Also serve with a fresh tossed salad.

Chicken Asparagus Soup

Excellent!

12	cups fat-free chicken broth	1	(15-ounce) can asparagus, cut into pieces
6	chicken breasts (skinless, boneless, with fat removed), chopped	1	teaspoon dried parsley
		1	teaspoon Cajun seasoning
1	(4 1/2-ounce) package cheddar broccoli rice & sauce mix (I use Lipton.)	3	bay leaves
			Salt, optional

- Spray a slow cooker with nonfat cooking spray.
- In the slow cooker mix together the broth, chicken breasts, rice and sauce mix, asparagus, parsley, Cajun seasoning, bay leaves, and salt, if using.
- Cover and cook on low for 9 hours.
- Remove the bay leaves before eating.

Yield: 20 (1-cup) servings

Calories: 78; Fat: 1g (10% fat); Cholesterol: 20mg; Carbohydrate: 6g; Dietary Fiber: 0g; Protein: 11g; Sodium: 456mg

 Menu idea: Serve this with Broccoli Ham & Cheese Frittata and Blueberry Crumb Cake, both found in *Busy People's Low-Fat Cookbook.*

Chicken Florentine Soup

This is a flavorful and low-calorie soup. It's great to have on hand when you're trying to lose a few extra pounds.

1 pound boneless, skinless chicken breasts, cut into tiny pieces	1 (16-ounce) can spinach
	1/2 tablespoon dried dill weed
8 cups chicken broth (made from bouillon is okay)	1 tablespoon lemon juice (bottled is fine)
1 (16-ounce) bag frozen mixed oriental vegetables	1 cup instant rice

- Spray a slow cooker with nonfat cooking spray.
- In the slow cooker mix together the chicken, broth, vegetables, spinach, dill weed, and lemon juice.
- Cover and cook on high for 5 hours.
- Stir in the instant rice.
- Cover and cook for 1/2 hour on high.
- Serve hot.

Yield: 10 (1-cup) servings

Calories: 140; Fat: 1g (9% fat); Cholesterol: 26mg; Carbohydrate: 15g; Dietary Fiber: 1g; Protein: 16g; Sodium: 669mg

 Menu idea: This hearty soup is a complete well-rounded meal and excellent source of low-fat carbohydrates.

Chicken Noodle Soup

Just assemble and let the slow cooker do all the work.

1½ pounds boneless, skinless chicken breasts, fat removed and cut into bite-size pieces	½ cup chopped celery
1 (49½-ounce) can fat-free chicken broth	2 small bay leaves or 1 large bay leaf
1 cup frozen cut carrots	2 cups home-style egg noodles, uncooked
½ cup frozen chopped onion	Salt and pepper, optional

- Spray a slow cooker with nonfat cooking spray.
- In the slow cooker mix together the chicken, broth, carrots, onion, celery, and bay leaf.
- Cover and cook on high for 4 hours or on low for 7 to 9 hours. (If cooking on low, turn the slow cooker on high for ½ hour before adding the noodles.)
- Stir in the noodles. (If desired skim off the top of the soup before adding the noodles, but it is not necessary.)
- Cover and cook on high an additional 10 to 12 minutes or until the noodles are "al dente" (tender). Do not overcook.
- Turn the slow cooker off.
- Remove the bay leaves.
- If desired, add salt and pepper to taste.
- Serve hot.

Note: To save preparation time simply purchase chicken breasts already cut up. Often butchers will label chicken breasts precut into little pieces as *stir-fry chicken.*

Yield: 9 (1-cup) servings

Calories: 137; Fat: 1g (9% fat); Cholesterol: 52mg; Carbohydrate: 9g; Dietary Fiber: 1g; Protein: 21g; Sodium: 375mg

 Menu idea: To complete this menu a fresh vegetable tray along with my creamy, smooth Vegetable Dip and Cheese Biscuits, both from *Busy People's Low-Fat Cookbook*, will satisfy the hungry tummies of your family.

Chunky Chili

Made with chunks of beef, the meat in this hearty chili is tenderized as it cooks.

1	pound stew meat (eye of round), cut into 1/2-inch chunks	1	(14 1/2-ounce) can diced low-sodium tomatoes
1	(15-ounce) can Mexican-style hot chili beans	1	(16-ounce) jar thick and chunky salsa
		1	tablespoon sugar

- Spray a slow cooker with nonfat cooking spray.
- Put into the slow cooker the meat, chili beans, tomatoes, salsa, and sugar and stir until well mixed.
- Cover and cook on low for 8 to 10 hours or on high for 4 to 5 hours.

Note: If desired, sprinkle each serving with nonfat shredded cheddar cheese. Let sit for 1 minute to let the cheese melt before serving.

Yield: 7 (1-cup) servings

Calories: 186; Fat: 5g (26% fat); Cholesterol: 40mg; Carbohydrate: 16g; Dietary Fiber: 3g; Protein: 16g; Sodium: 569mg

 Menu idea: Serve with the Sweet Corn Bread (page 41) and a fresh vegetable tray with fat-free vegetable dip.

Vegetarian Chili

This chili is so thick and filling, no one would ever miss the meat or know it was vegetarian.

2	(15-ounce) cans Mexican-style hot chili beans
1	(16-ounce) can vegetarian refried beans
1	(15-ounce) can black beans
2	cups chunky salsa
1	(6-ounce) can tomato paste
1	pound meatless ground burger (I use Morningstar Farms.)
1	(1.25-ounce) package taco seasoning mix

- Spray a slow cooker with nonfat cooking spray.
- In the cooker stir together the chili beans, refried beans, black beans, salsa, tomato paste, meatless ground burger, and seasoning until well mixed.
- Cover and cook on high for 2 to 3 hours or on low for 6 to 8 hours.

Yield: 13 (1-cup) servings

Calories: 186; Fat: 1g (5% fat); Cholesterol: 0mg; Carbohydrate: 28g; Dietary Fiber: 8g; Protein: 14g; Sodium: 1024mg

 Menu idea: If you serve this with Sweet Corn Bread (page 41), people will be surprised when they hear the entire meal was prepared in a slow cooker.

Cream of Broccoli & Mushroom Soup

This thick, rich soup will stick to your bones but not your hips, thighs, or arteries.

8	ounces fresh mushrooms, sliced	3	bay leaves
2	(1-pound) bags frozen broccoli stems and pieces	1	pint fat-free half-and-half
3	(10³/₄-ounce) cans 98 percent fat-free cream of broccoli soup	4	ounces extra-lean smoked ham, cut into tiny pieces
¹/₂	teaspoon dried thyme leaves, crushed		

- Spray a slow cooker with nonfat cooking spray.
- Put into the slow cooker the mushrooms, broccoli, soup, thyme, bay leaves, half-and-half, and ham. Mix well.
- Cover and cook on low for 8 to 9 hours or on high for 3¹/₂ to 4 hours.

Note: Remove the bay leaves before eating.

Yield: 12 (1-cup) servings

Calories: 112; Fat: 3g (18% fat); Cholesterol: 7mg; Carbohydrate: 17g; Dietary Fiber: 3g; Protein: 9g; Sodium: 629mg

 Menu idea: The Tangy Tossed Salad and the Pinwheel Dinner Rolls from *Busy People's Low-Fat Cookbook* nicely complement this recipe.

Fill-Me-Up Vegetable Soup

This came to me from Mary Pat White from my hometown of Swanton, Ohio. She says, "This is a good 'filler' for dieters; it warms you up and fills you up." With so many good vegetables it's practically a "freebie." Gets me through rough "I'm starving" days.

1 **(46-ounce) can vegetable juice**	1 **medium onion, diced, or 1 cup frozen chopped onion**
1 **small cabbage, shredded, or 1 pound packaged, ready-to-use coleslaw**	2 **cups frozen French-cut green beans**
1 **green pepper, diced, or 1 cup frozen chopped green peppers**	6 **teaspoons chicken bouillon**
3 **ribs celery, diced**	1 **teaspoon garlic powder, or use fresh garlic**

- Spray a slow cooker with nonfat cooking spray.
- In the slow cooker mix together the vegetable juice, cabbage, green pepper, celery, onion, green beans, chicken bouillon, and garlic powder.
- Cover and cook on low for 8 hours or on high for 4 hours.

Note: If you want to have thicker soup, put a few cups into the blender, vegetables and all, blend, and then return the mix to the pot.

Yield: 12 (1-cup) servings

Calories: 65; Fat: 0g (0% fat); Cholesterol: 0mg; Carbohydrate: 13g; Dietary fiber: 3g; Protein: 2g; Sodium: 899mg

 Menu idea: Served with Cheese Biscuits and Apple Oatmeal Cookies, both from *Busy People's Low-Fat Cookbook,* this is a satisfying meal.

Green Bean Soup

This is one of my favorite soups. I got the idea from a high-fat soup served at one of the restaurants where I used to work.

1 (14-ounce) package low-fat smoked sausage, cut into bite-size pieces	1 pound frozen cut green beans
¼ cup Butter Buds Sprinkles	8 cups chicken stock (or 8 cups water with 8 chicken bouillon cubes, dissolved)
1 cup frozen chopped onion or 1 medium onion, chopped	4 whole dried bay leaves
1 pound frozen hash browns (tiny cubes)	

- Spray a slow cooker with nonfat cooking spray.
- Put into the slow cooker the sausage, Butter Buds, onion, hash browns, green beans, chicken stock, and bay leaves and stir until well mixed.
- Cover and cook on low for 8 to 10 hours or on for high 4 to 5 hours.
- Remove the bay leaves before eating.

Yield: 12 (1-cup) servings

Calories: 107; Fat: 1g (8% fat); Cholesterol: 12mg; Carbohydrate: 17g; Dietary Fiber: 2g; Protein: 8g; Sodium: 717mg

 Menu idea: Serve this with Tomato Biscuits from *Busy People's Low-Fat Cookbook.*

New-Fashioned Vegetable Soup

This soup is chock full of delicious nutrition.

I	(46-ounce) can vegetable juice	I	(16-ounce) bag coleslaw mix
I	(12-ounce) bag meatless ground burger, crumbled (I use Morningstar Farms.)	I	onion, chopped
		2	pounds frozen mixed vegetables

- Spray a slow cooker with nonfat cooking spray.
- In the slow cooker mix together the vegetable juice, burger, coleslaw, onion, and mixed vegetables.
- Cover and cook on high for 8 to 10 hours.

Yield: 13 (1-cup) servings

Calories: 48; Fat: 0g (0% fat); Cholesterol: 0mg; Carbohydrate: 8g; Dietary Fiber: 2g; Protein: 4g; Sodium: 170mg

 Menu idea: Serve this soup with the Cranberry Apple Salad and the Pinwheel Dinner Rolls, both from *Busy People's Low-Fat Cookbook*.

Pizza Soup

This soup is easily put together in a snap.

1 (14-ounce) jar pizza sauce	1 (26-ounce) can condensed tomato soup
½ cup frozen chopped onion, or fresh onion	1 (26-ounce) can water
1 (4-ounce) can sliced mushrooms, drained	4 ounces fat-free mozzarella cheese
1 ounce thinly sliced pepperoni, cut into tiny strips	

- Spray a slow cooker with nonfat cooking spray.
- In the slow cooker mix together the pizza sauce, onion, mushrooms, pepperoni, tomato soup, and water.
- Cover and cook on high for 4 hours or on low for 8 hours.
- Garnish each serving with mozzarella cheese.
- Serve hot.

Yield: 7 (1-cup) servings

Calories: 144; Fat: 2g (11% fat); Cholesterol: 5mg; Carbohydrate: 22g; Dietary Fiber: 3g; Protein: 9g; Sodium: 1196mg

 Menu idea: The Chocolate Cheese Squares from *Busy People's Low-Fat Cookbook* will complete this easy-to-prepare meal.

Smokey Bean Soup

There's nothing like comin' home to the wonderful aroma of this mouth-watering soup.

1 (48-ounce) jar deluxe mixed beans	1 teaspoon liquid smoke (found in sauce aisle of grocery store)
48 ounces water	1 (1½-ounce) package dry onion soup mix
1 (16-ounce) bag frozen vegetables for stew (I use Freshlike.)	¾ teaspoon dried thyme, optional
¾ pound smoked, lean, ham or turkey ham, chopped	

- Spray a slow cooker with nonfat cooking spray.
- Put the beans into the slow cooker.
- With a potato masher, mash the beans until at least one-third are mashed.
- Fill the bean jar you just emptied with the water and add it to the slow cooker.
- Add the frozen vegetables. (Note: I like to remove the peas from the frozen vegetables first.)
- Add the ham, liquid smoke, soup mix, water, and thyme, if using.
- Stir until well mixed and the dry onion soup mix is completely dissolved.
- Cover and cook on low for 8 to 10 hours.
- Before serving, if you want the broth thicker, simply mash the soup with the potato masher again.
- Stir and serve hot.

Note: The soup actually needs only 5 hours on low in the slow cooker before it's ready to eat. It's hard to overcook this soup, so don't worry if it's in the slow cooker for longer than 10 hours.

Yield: 15 (1-cup) servings

Calories: 137; Fat: 2g (11% fat); Cholesterol: 7mg; Carbohydrate: 20g; Dietary Fiber: 8g; Protein: 10g; Sodium: 851mg

 Menu idea: The easy-to-make and delicious Mexican Cheese Moons from *Busy People's Low-Fat Cookbook* are a terrific flavor combination with this soup.

Southwestern Vegetarian Soup

This soup is especially good on a cold winter day.

6 cups chicken broth (6 bouillon cubes with 6 cups water)	1 (1-pound) package frozen vegetables (I use Freshlike.)
2 cups salsa	1 (16-ounce) can fat-free refried beans
1 (1¼-ounce) package taco seasoning	

- Spray a slow cooker with nonfat cooking spray.
- In the slow cooker mix together the broth, salsa, taco seasoning, vegetables, and refried beans.
- Cover and cook on low for 8 hours or on high for 4 hours.
- If desired, sprinkle crushed baked tortilla chips on individual servings of soup before eating. For a spicier soup add a few drops of hot sauce.

Yield: 12 (1-cup) servings

Calories: 86; Fat: 0g (0% fat); Cholesterol: 0mg; Carbohydrate: 15g; Dietary Fiber: 2g; Protein: 3g; Sodium: 851mg

 Menu idea: I love serving this for multiple course meals. It goes great with a meat-and-potato entrée.

Split Pea Soup

This soup is hearty, thick, and flavorful. (A large slow cooker is needed for this recipe.)

4 (14-ounce) cans fat-free chicken broth	1½ pounds extra lean smoked ham, cut into tiny cubes
2 cups fat-free frozen hash browns (chopped, not the shredded style)	1 (1-pound) bag dry split peas
	½ teaspoon dried thyme
1 cup frozen chopped onion	1 (15-ounce) can sliced carrots, drained

- Spray a slow cooker with nonfat cooking spray.
- In the slow cooker mix together the broth, hash browns, onion, ham, peas, and thyme.
- Cover and cook on low for 10 to 12 hours.
- Stir in the carrots.
- Cover and cook for 5 more minutes or until the carrots are heated.

Yield: 12 (1-cup) servings

Calories: 240; Fat: 3g (12% fat); Cholesterol: 27mg; Carbohydrate: 30g; Dietary Fiber: 11g; Protein: 23g; Sodium: 1148mg

 Menu idea: Tomato Biscuits and a fresh vegetable served with my homemade Vegetable Dip, both from *Busy People's Low-Fat Cookbook*, complete this all-time favorite comfort food.

Steak & Potato Cattlemen's Soup

This is a terrific way to use leftover steak and potatoes or an eye of round roast and potatoes.

2¹/₂ cups (I pound) leftover cooked eye of round steak, cut into bite-size chunks

2¹/₂ cups (2 large potatoes) leftover, fully cooked potatoes (with skins on), cut into bite-size chunks

4 ounces fresh sliced mushrooms

¹/₂ cup barbecue sauce

¹/₂ cup chopped onions (frozen onions work well)

I (I¹/₄-ounce) envelope dry onion soup mix

4 cups water

- Spray a slow cooker with nonfat cooking spray.
- In the slow cooker combine the steak, potatoes, mushrooms, barbecue sauce, onions, soup mix, and water and mix well.
- Cover and cook on low for 4 hours.

Yield: 6 (1-cup) servings

Calories: 235; Fat: 4g (17% fat); Cholesterol: 52mg; Carbohydrate: 23g; Dietary Fiber: 3g; Protein: 25g; Sodium: 752mg

 Menu idea: I like serving this in the early spring, fall, and winter months with other comfort foods such as the Pumpkin Apple Bake from *Busy People's Low-Fat Cookbook* and Sweet Corn Bread (page 41).

Taco Vegetable Soup

My family thinks this flavorful, zesty soup is delicious served with crushed, baked tortilla chips sprinkled on top of each serving.

I pound ground turkey breast	I (49½-ounce) can chicken broth, floating fat removed
2 (16-ounce) bags frozen vegetables	I (16-ounce) jar salsa (I use Tostitos.)
I (1¼-ounce) package taco seasoning	Baked tortilla chips, optional
	Tabasco, optional

- Spray a slow cooker with nonfat cooking spray.
- In the slow cooker mix together the turkey, vegetables, taco seasoning, broth, and salsa.
- Cover and cook on low for 8 hours.
- If desired serve with crushed, baked tortilla chips sprinkled on top of each serving. If you like a spicier soup, add a few drops of Tabasco.

Yield: 12 (1-cup) servings

Calories: 118; Fat: 0g (0% fat); Cholesterol: 26mg; Carbohydrate: 14g; Dietary Fiber: 0g; Protein: 11g; Sodium: 740mg

 Menu idea: For a zesty meal prepare Mexican Cheese Moons from *Busy People's Low-Fat Cookbook* and serve with this dish.

World's Easiest Vegetable Soup

There's nothin' like a hot bowl of soup on a cold wintry day, and this one is perfect.

1 (46-ounce) can vegetable juice	4 (15¼-ounce) cans mixed vegetables, drained
4 cups fat-free beef broth (made from beef bouillon is fine)	1 teaspoon salad seasoning (I use Durkee, but Mrs. Dash will work.)

- Spray a slow cooker with nonfat cooking spray.
- In the slow cooker mix together the vegetable juice, broth, vegetables, and spices.
- Cover and cook on low for 4 hours or on high for 2 hours.

Yield: 16 (1-cup) servings

Calories: 61; Fat: 0g (0% fat); Cholesterol: 0mg; Carbohydrate: 11g; Dietary Fiber: 3g; Protein: 3g; Sodium: 552mg

★ **Beef Vegetable Soup:** Make exactly like vegetable soup but add 2 pounds of eye of round beef cut into bite-size pieces. (No need to precook. The meat will cook while boiling.)

Yield: 20 (1-cup) Beef Vegetable Soup servings

Calories: 109; Fat: 2g (20% fat); Cholesterol: 24mg; Carbohydrate: 9g; Dietary Fiber: 2g; Protein: 12g; Sodium: 446mg

Menu idea: Serve this soup with a Ham & Cheese Omelet and Tiny Turnovers, both found in *Busy People's Low-Fat Cookbook*.

Three Bean & Ham Soup

This soup is a great source of protein and has excellent flavor.

I	(16-ounce) can pork and beans	I	(10½-ounce) can condensed tomato soup
I	(15½-ounce) can lima beans		
I	(15½-ounce) can mild chili beans	I	(I-ounce) envelope dry onion soup mix (2 envelopes per box)
I	pound lean ham, cubed	4	cups hot water

- Spray a slow cooker with nonfat cooking spray.
- Pour the cans of pork and beans, lima beans, and chili beans into the slow cooker.
- With a hand-held mixer beat the beans in the slow cooker on high speed for 1 minute to make a thick base for the soup.
- Add the cubed ham, tomato soup, onion soup mix, and water.
- Stir until well mixed.
- Cover and cook on high for 2 to 3 hours or on low for 4 to 6 hours.

Yield: 10 (1-cup) servings

Calories: 201; Fat: 3g (15% fat); Cholesterol: 25mg; Carbohydrate: 28g; Dietary Fiber: 6g; Protein: 16g; Sodium: 1682mg

 Menu idea: The Parmesan Garlic Quick Bread (page 38) served with the Sassy Slaw from *Busy People's Low-Fat Cookbook* are tasty side dishes that complement this delightful meal with convenience for the cook.

Tomato Bisque

So much more special than traditional, plain ol' tomato soup. This recipe was created by Ted Eagle of Wall, Pennsylvania. Thanks, Ted.

1 **(26-ounce) can condensed tomato soup**	1 **(14¹/₂-ounce) can low-sodium diced tomatoes or 3 plum tomatoes, skinned and chopped**
13 **ounces water**	1 **cup fat-free half-and-half**

- Spray a slow cooker with nonfat cooking spray.
- In the slow cooker mix together the tomato soup, water, tomatoes, and half-and-half.
- Cover and cook on high for 2 hours or on low for 4 to 6 hours.
- Serve hot.

Yield: 7 (1-cup) servings

Calories: 102; Fat: 0g (0% fat); Cholesterol: 0mg; Carbohydrate: 22g; Dietary Fiber: 2g; Protein: 5g; Sodium: 660mg

 Menu idea: This soup is great served with Low-Fat Grilled Cheese Sandwiches, Spiced Tea, and Very Berry Fruit Salad, all found in *Busy People's Low-Fat Cookbook.*

Unstuffed Cabbage Soup

If you like stuffed cabbage rolls, you'll like this. It's a lot faster and easier to prepare than Cabbage Rolls.

1	pound ground eye of round beef	2	cups frozen chopped onion, or 2 cups fresh
6	cups beef broth (made with bouillon is okay)	1	(1-pound) bag coleslaw mix, or 10 cups shredded fresh green cabbage
4	cups low-sodium vegetable juice	2	cups instant rice
2	(14½-ounce) cans stewed tomatoes		

- Spray a slow cooker with nonfat cooking spray.
- In the slow cooker mix together the beef, broth, vegetable juice, tomatoes, onion, and coleslaw.
- Cover and cook on low for 8 to 10 hours or on high for 4 to 5 hours.
- Before serving stir in the rice.
- Cover and let the soup sit for 5 minutes.
- Serve hot.

Yield: 16 (1-cup) servings

Calories: 140; Fat: 3g (20% fat); Cholesterol: 10mg; Carbohydrate: 18g; Dietary Fiber: 2g; Protein: 9g; Sodium: 488mg

 Menu idea: The Sweet and Sour Fresh Vegetable Garden Salad with crackers and the Zucchini Snack Cake, both from *Busy People's Low-Fat Cookbook*, make this a meal worth remembering.

Unstuffed Green Pepper Soup

If you like stuffed green peppers, give this a try. You'll love it, and it's so much quicker and easier to prepare than Stuffed Green Peppers.

1/2 pound ground eye of round beef	1 cup frozen chopped green peppers or 1 cup fresh
3 cups fat-free beef broth (made with bouillon is okay)	1 cup frozen chopped onion or 1 cup fresh
2 cups or 3 (5 1/2-ounce) cans low-sodium vegetable juice	1 cup instant rice
2 (14 1/2-ounce) cans stewed tomatoes	

- Spray a large slow cooker with nonfat cooking spray.
- In the slow cooker mix together the beef, broth, vegetable juice, tomatoes, green peppers, and onion.
- Cover and cook on low for 8 to 10 hours or on high for 4 to 5 hours.
- Before serving stir in the rice. Cover and let sit for 5 minutes.
- Serve hot.

Yield: 8 (1-cup) servings

Calories: 151; Fat: 3g (19% fat); Cholesterol: 10mg; Carbohydrate: 21g; Dietary Fiber: 2g; Protein: 9g; Sodium: 593mg

 Menu idea: Serve this with Cheese Biscuits and Peaches and Cream Gelatin Salad, both found in *Busy People's Low-Fat Cookbook*.

Vegetable Hobo Soup

This is a great soup for dieters—full of nutrition, low in calories, and no fat.

3	pounds frozen mixed vegetables		Salt
			Garlic powder
1	(46-ounce) can vegetable juice	1	(16-ounce) package coleslaw
2	bay leaves		mix

- Spray a slow cooker with nonfat cooking spray.
- In the slow cooker mix together the vegetables, vegetable juice, bay leaves, salt and garlic powder to taste, and coleslaw.
- Cover and cook on low for 8 to 10 hours.
- Remove the bay leaves before serving.

Yield: 13 (1-cup) servings

Calories: 43; Fat: 0g (0% fat); Cholesterol: 0mg; Carbohydrate: 9g; Dietary Fiber: 2g; Protein: 2g; Sodium: 145mg

 Menu idea: The Cheese Biscuits and Apple Berry Bake, both from the *Busy People's Low-Fat Cookbook*, turn this hearty soup into a hearty meal.

Clam Chowder

There's no way people would ever know this is low-fat if you don't tell them. It's super thick, rich, and creamy.

3 **(10³/₄-ounce) cans 98% fat-free cream of celery soup**	1 **(1-pound) bag frozen, fat-free shredded hash brown potatoes**
2 **(6¹/₂-ounce) cans chopped clams, not drained**	¹/₂ **cup frozen chopped onion**
	1 **pint fat-free half-and-half**

- Spray a slow cooker with nonfat cooking spray.
- Put into the slow cooker the soup, clams, hash brown potatoes, onion, and half-and-half.
- Stir until well mixed.
- Cover and cook on low for 8 to 9 hours.

Yield: 11 (1-cup) servings

Calories: 129; Fat: 2g (13% fat); Cholesterol: 15mg; Carbohydrate: 22g; Dietary Fiber: 2g; Protein: 8g; Sodium: 785mg

 Menu idea: This is great served with Sassy Slaw from *Busy People's Low-Fat Cookbook.*

Corn Chowder

Even picky eaters like this special chowder.

2/3 cup fat-free shredded cheddar cheese	1 (14^1/2-ounce) can clear chicken broth
1 teaspoon onion salt	^{1}/4 teaspoon ground pepper, optional
1 (11-ounce) can sweet corn and diced peppers	
2 (15-ounce) cans of cream-style corn	

- Spray a slow cooker with nonfat cooking spray.
- In the slow cooker mix together the cheese, onion salt, corn and peppers, corn, chicken broth, and pepper, if desired.
- Cover and cook on low for 6 hours.

Yield: 6 (1-cup) servings

Calories: 167; Fat: 1g (4% fat); Cholesterol: 1mg; Carbohydrate: 36g; Dietary Fiber: 3g; Protein: 9g; Sodium: 1131mg

 Menu idea: I like serving this during the holidays with lean ham or turkey along with some of my family's other favorites such as the Peachy Pumpkin Bread (page 39).

Ham & Bean Chowder

Two thumbs up for this delicious use of canned pork and beans.

2   (16-ounce) cans pork and beans
1   (10³/4-ounce) can condensed tomato soup
1   pound extra lean smoked ham, cut into ¹/2-inch cubes
¹/3 cup chopped onion (about half a small onion)

2   (14¹/2-ounce) cans stewed tomatoes
¹/2 cup Mueller's brand elbow macaroni, dry

- Spray a slow cooker with nonfat cooking spray.
- Discard any fat you see in the pork and beans before pouring them into the slow cooker.
- Mash the beans for a couple of minutes with either a potato masher or slotted spoon to make a thicker broth.
- Stir in the tomato soup, ham, onion, and stewed tomatoes.
- Cover and cook on high for 4 to 5 hours or on low for 9 to 10 hours.
- If cooking on low, turn the temperature up to high. (If cooking on high, it will already be boiling.) Once the broth starts to boil, add the pasta. Cover and continue cooking on high for an additional 25 to 30 minutes or until pasta is tender.

Yield: 9 (1-cup) servings

Calories: 236; Fat: 4g (14% fat); Cholesterol: 31mg; Carbohydrate: 36g; Dietary Fiber: 7g; Protein: 17g; Sodium: 1566mg

 Menu idea: Serving the Sweet Corn Bread (page 41) with the Spring Salad, from *Busy People's Low-Fat Cookbook*, is an excellent flavor combination with this stick-to-your-ribs, but not your hips or thighs, soup.

Mushroom Chowder

This thick, creamy, buttery comfort food makes you feel warm and good inside with every bite.

8	cups water	1¹/₂	pounds fresh sliced mushrooms
8	chicken bouillon cubes	4	ounces chopped smoked lean ham
1	tablespoon minced garlic (I use the kind in the jar.)		
2	(¹/₂-ounce) packets Butter Buds Mix, or 2 tablespoons Butter Buds Sprinkles, dry	3	(2-ounce) packages instant mashed potatoes, dry—do not make as directed

- Spray a slow cooker with nonfat cooking spray.
- In the slow cooker mix together the water, bouillon cubes, garlic, Butter Buds, mushrooms, and ham.
- Cover and cook on high for 2 hours.
- Stir in the instant mashed potatoes one packet at a time.
- Serve immediately.

Yield: 10 (1-cup) servings

Calories: 109; Fat: 1g (6% fat); Cholesterol: 6mg; Carbohydrate: 20g; Dietary Fiber: 2g; Protein: 7g; Sodium: 1225mg

 Menu idea: This is great served with Sweet & Sour Fresh Vegetable Garden Salad from *Busy People's Low-Fat Cookbook.*

Potato Chowder

This chowder is a great way to use leftover baked potatoes.

1/4 cup all-purpose flour	1/2 teaspoon dried dill weed
1 quart fat-free non-dairy creamer	Pinch of ground black pepper
8 ounces fat-free shredded cheddar cheese	6 cups cubed potatoes
5 tablespoons imitation bacon bits	Salt and pepper, optional

- Spray a slow cooker with nonfat cooking spray.
- In the slow cooker stir together with a whisk the flour and non-dairy creamer until the flour is dissolved.
- Add the cheese, bacon bits, dill weed, black pepper, and potatoes.
- Stir until well mixed. Cover and cook on low for 8 to 10 hours.
- Remove 2 cups of the potatoes and 1 cup of the broth and put them into a blender.
- Pulse the blender for short periods of time until the potatoes are smooth, thick, and creamy.
- Put the potatoes back into the slow cooker and stir until well mixed.
- Cover and cook for another 15 to 20 minutes.
- If desired, sprinkle more finely shredded cheddar cheese on each serving.
- Add salt and pepper to taste.

Yield: 7 (1-cup) servings

Calories: 403; Fat: 1g (2% fat); Cholesterol: 3mg; Carbohydrate: 74g; Dietary Fiber: 2g; Protein: 13g; Sodium: 317mg

 Menu idea: Serve this with Bacon Lettuce and Tomato Salad from *Busy People's Low-Fat Cookbook.*

Taco Chowder

Great served on a chilly rainy night. It'll warm you from head to toe.

1	pound ground meatless burger (I use Morningstar Farms.)	1	(14½-ounce) can fat-free beef broth
1	(1¼-ounce) packet taco seasoning	1	(15-ounce) can light red kidney beans, not drained
1	(28-ounce) can diced tomatoes, not drained	1	(15¼-ounce) can whole kernel golden sweet corn, not drained
2	(16-ounce) cans fat-free refried beans		

- Spray a slow cooker with nonfat cooking spray.
- In the slow cooker mix together the meatless ground burger, taco seasoning, tomatoes, refried beans, beef broth, kidney beans, and corn.
- Cover and cook on high for 4 to 5 hours or on low for 8 to 10 hours.
- If desired, sprinkle the chowder lightly with fat-free cheddar cheese or crushed baked tortilla chips.

Yield: 13 (1-cup) servings

Calories: 172; Fat: 1g (3% fat); Cholesterol: 0mg; Carbohydrate: 28g; Dietary Fiber: 8g; Protein: 14g; Sodium: 904mg

 Menu idea: This is good served with Mexican Chicken Salad from *Busy People's Low-Fat Cookbook.*

Southwestern Three Beans

This salad has zip.

- 1 (19-ounce) can black bean soup, drained
- 1/2 cup red wine vinegar salad dressing
- 1 (15 1/2-ounce) can light red kidney beans, drained
- 1 (15 1/2-ounce) can navy beans, drained
- 1 (16-ounce) jar chunky salsa Tabasco, optional

- Spray a slow cooker with nonfat cooking spray.
- Put the black bean soup, salad dressing, kidney beans, navy beans, and salsa into the slow cooker. If you like spicy food add a few drops of Tabasco.
- Cover and cook on low for 8 hours.

Yield: 12 (1/2-cup) servings

Calories: 112; Fat: 0g (0% fat); Cholesterol: 0mg; Carbohydrate: 19g; Dietary Fiber: 5g; Protein: 6g; Sodium: 645mg

 Menu idea: Use any leftovers as a salad. Add 1 medium onion, chopped, and chill. It's also great served as a hot dip.

Seafood Chowder

This is an elaborate chowder that is definitely for a special meal.

1 pint fat-free half-and-half	1 (8-ounce) package imitation crab
1 (6-ounce) package small shrimp	
2 (6½-ounce) cans minced clams, not drained	3 (10¾-ounce) cans fat-free New England clam chowder
1 (8-ounce) package imitation scallops, cut into bite-size pieces	1 pound fat-free frozen hash browns
	Pepper, optional

- Spray a slow cooker with nonfat cooking spray.
- In the slow cooker mix together the half-and-half, shrimp, clams, scallops, crab, chowder, and hash browns.
- Cover and cook on low for 8 to 9 hours or on high for 4 hours.
- If desired, add pepper to taste before serving.

Yield: 10 (1-cup) servings

Calories: 217; Fat: 2g (9% fat); Cholesterol: 59mg; Carbohydrate: 32g; Dietary Fiber: 2g; Protein: 19g; Sodium: 1335mg

 Menu idea: This rich, creamy chowder gets extra "wow" reviews when served with sourdough bread rolls and a crispy Caesar salad, made with fat-free dressing, of course.

Seafood Pasta

This is truly a seafood lover's delight.

I recipe Seafood Chowder (opposite page), omitting hash browns	Ground black pepper, optional
	Fat-free grated Parmesan cheese, for garnish
I pound dry spaghetti or linguine (Mueller's brand), cooked as directed	

- Make the Seafood Chowder recipe, leaving out the hash browns.
- Serve over the cooked pasta.
- If desired, sprinkle with ground black pepper before serving.
- Serve with fat-free, grated Parmesan cheese on the side

Yield: 8 servings (1 cup sauce and 1 cup cooked pasta)

Calories: 433; Fat: 4g (8% fat); Cholesterol: 74mg; Carbohydrate: 71g; Dietary Fiber: 2g; Protein: 29g; Sodium: 1656mg

 Menu idea: If you are a seafood lover (like me) then you'll like serving this recipe with the Seaside Salad along with the easy to make Garlic Toast, both from *Busy People's Low-Fat Cookbook*.

Hot, Not Fat, Fruit Salad

This hot fruit salad tastes especially good served over angel food cake or frozen fat-free ice cream.

I (20-ounce) can pineapple	I (20-ounce) can light cherry pie filling
I (20-ounce) can pears	
I (20-ounce) can peaches	$^3/_4$ cup brown sugar
I (20-ounce) can apricots	I pound fat-free margarine

- Spray a slow cooker with nonfat cooking spray.
- In the slow cooker mix together the pineapple, pears, peaches, apricots, cherry pie filling, sugar, and margarine.
- Cover and cook on high for 1½ to 2 hours or on low for 4 hours.

Yield: 30 (½-cup) servings

Calories: 67; Fat: 0g (0% fat); Cholesterol: 0mg; Carbohydrate: 16g; Dietary Fiber: 1g; Protein: 0g; Sodium: 105mg

 Menu idea: This concoction is good served on fat-free ice cream, fat-free frozen yogurt, or on sliced angel food cake.

Hot Potato Salad

People often request this recipe.

4	large potatoes (about 2 pounds) with skins, cut into I-inch chunks	$^1/_4$	cup fresh chopped chives
I	tablespoon minced garlic (I use the kind in a jar.)	4	ounces fat-free shredded cheddar cheese
$^3/_4$	cup red wine vinegar salad dressing	I	(3-ounce) jar real bacon bits

- Spray a slow cooker with nonfat cooking spray.
- In the slow cooker mix together the potatoes, garlic, dressing, and chives.
- Cover and cook on high for 5 hours.
- Add the cheese and bacon bits 10 minutes before serving.

Yield: 14 ($^1/_2$-cup) servings

Calories: 100; Fat: 1g (12% fat); Cholesterol: 6mg; Carbohydrate: 16g; Dietary fiber: 1g; Protein: 6g; Sodium: 447mg

 Menu idea: This is good served with Chicken Nuggets from *Busy People's Low-Fat Cookbook.*

Tropical Cabbage

My secret ingredients turn regular cabbage into an extra special surprise.

1 **(16-ounce) package ready-to-use coleslaw**	³/₄ **cup low-fat slaw dressing (I use Marzetti.)**
1 **(20-ounce) can crushed pineapple with juice (Discard 1 cup of juice.)**	¹/₂ **teaspoon ground cinnamon**
	1 **pound extra lean ham, cubed**

- Spray a slow cooker with nonfat cooking spray.
- In the slow cooker mix together the coleslaw, pineapple, pineapple juice, slaw dressing, cinnamon, and ham.
- Cover and cook on low for 8 hours or on high for 4 hours.

Yield: 10 (½-cup) servings

Calories: 120; Fat: 2g (18% fat); Cholesterol: 30mg; Carbohydrate: 15g; Dietary Fiber: 1g; Protein: 9g; Sodium: 898mg

 Menu idea: Serve this with Sweet Corn Bread (page 41) and any protein such as grilled chicken, fish, pork, or beef tenderloin to make a well rounded and flavorful meal.

Warm Barbecue Bean Salad

These beans get gobbled up quickly.

$^3/_4$ cup barbecue sauce	1 (15$^1/_2$-ounce) can shoe-peg corn, drained
2 (16-ounce) cans baked beans, drained	1 medium sweet red pepper, chopped
1 cup frozen chopped onion or 1 medium-size fresh onion, chopped	1 tablespoon brown sugar
	1 (3-ounce) jar real bacon bits

- Spray a slow cooker with nonfat cooking spray.
- In the slow cooker mix together the barbecue sauce, baked beans, onion, corn, red pepper, sugar, and bacon bits.
- Cover and cook on low for 8 hours.

Yield: 10 ($^1/_2$-cup) servings

Calories: 172; Fat: 3g (13% fat); Cholesterol: 6mg; Carbohydrate: 31g; Dietary Fiber: 6g; Protein: 9g; Sodium: 877mg

 Menu idea: This is a great dish for potlucks, cookouts, and picnics.

Warm Cranberry Apple Salad

A terrific substitute for the traditional cranberries served during the holidays.

I	(21-ounce) can apple pie filling	I	teaspoon cinnamon
I	(16-ounce) can whole-berry cranberry sauce		

- Spray a slow cooker with nonfat cooking spray.
- When you open the can of apple pie filling, insert a sharp knife into the can and cut the apples into small pieces.
- In the slow cooker mix together the apple pie filling, cranberry sauce, and cinnamon.
- Cover and cook on low for 4 hours.

Yield: 8 (½-cup) servings

Calories: 157; Fat: 0g (0% fat); Cholesterol: 0mg; Carbohydrate: 41g; Dietary Fiber: 2g; Protein: 0g; Sodium: 45mg

 Menu idea: Great on its own or as a topping for a low-fat cake.

Side Dishes

> **He who is good at making excuses
> is seldom good for anything else.**

Asparagus

Usually fresh asparagus is expensive, but when it's on sale, I love to make this recipe. It's so good.

1	(14¹/₂-ounce) can fat-free chicken broth
1	tablespoon Butter Buds Sprinkles
¹/₂	teaspoon garlic salt
2	pounds fresh asparagus, cleaned and about 1¹/₂ inches cut off the bottoms*

- Spray a slow cooker with nonfat cooking spray.
- In a slow cooker stir together the chicken broth, Butter Buds Sprinkles, and garlic salt until dissolved.
- Put the fresh asparagus into the slow cooker. The asparagus does not need to be fully submerged in the broth. The steam will cook the asparagus.
- Cover and cook on low for 6 to 8 hours.

*Note: You may need to cut the asparagus in half to fit in the slow cooker. Using an oval shaped slow cooker was good for me because I was able to cook the fresh asparagus in whole spears.

Yield: 8 (¹/₄-pound) servings

Calories: 37; Fat: 0g (0% fat); Cholesterol: 0mg; Carbohydrate: 6g; Dietary Fiber: 2g; Protein: 3g; Sodium: 260mg

 Menu idea: This is good with any entrée served warm, such as the Hearty Barbecue Skillet Dinner from *Busy People's Low-Fat Cookbook*.

Apple-Yam Casserole

Perfect! This casserole is a cross between apple pie and sweet potato pie.

1	**(20-ounce) can apple pie filling**	1 **(24-ounce) can yams, drained**
1/2	**teaspoon cinnamon**	**and cut into bite-size pieces**
2	**tablespoons brown sugar**	**Dash of salt, optional**

- Spray a slow cooker with nonfat cooking spray.
- Open the can of apple pie filling, insert a sharp knife into the can, and cut the apples in the pie filling into bite-size pieces.
- In the slow cooker mix together the filling, cinnamon, brown sugar, yams, and salt, if using.
- Cover and cook on high for 2 hours or on low for 4 to 8 hours.
- Serve warm.

Note: You can also make this as a pocket pouch (page 6).

Yield: 12 (½-cup) servings

Calories: 80; Fat: 0g (0% fat); Cholesterol: 0mg; Carbohydrate: 19g; Dietary Fiber: 2g; Protein: 1g; Sodium: 49mg

 Menu idea: Great for Thanksgiving or Christmas or with lean pork entrées such as Pork Tenderloin (page 172).

Apricot Sweet Potatoes

This flavor combination tastes wonderful with pork tenderloin or lean ham steaks.

1 (40-ounce) can cut sweet potatoes (yams) in light syrup, drained	⅓ cup apricot preserves with no large chunks of apricots

- Spray a slow cooker with nonfat cooking spray.
- In the slow cooker mix together the sweet potatoes (yams) with the apricot preserves until it is the consistency of thick mashed potatoes, *but* with large chunks.
- Cook on low for 6 hours.

Note: You can also make this as a pocket pouch (page 6).

Yield: 8 (½-cup) servings

Calories: 175; Fat: 0g (0% fat); Cholesterol: 0mg; Carbohydrate: 41g; Dietary Fiber: 3g; Protein: 3g; Sodium: 112mg

 Menu idea: When served with a green vegetable side dish such as Mushroom, Onion & Bacon Green Bean Casserole from *Busy People's Low-Fat Cookbook* and lean pork, you have a complete meal.

Baked Potatoes

This is a "no-brainer" recipe, meaning you could probably do it with your eyes shut and your hands tied behind your back.

6 to 8 medium potatoes, washed

- Prick the potatoes with a fork.
- Wrap each potato individually in foil and put them in the slow cooker.
- Cover and cook on high for 3 to 4½ hours or on low for 7 to 10 hours.

Yield: 6 to 8 servings

Calories: 100; Fat: 0g (0% fat); Cholesterol: 0mg; Carbohydrate: 26g; Dietary Fiber: 3g; Protein: 4g; Sodium: 0mg

 Menu idea: These potatoes are good with any lean meat, chicken, or fish entrée along with a green vegetable.

Baked Sweet Potatoes

Slow cooking these enhances the sweet potatoes' flavor. I love to serve them with brown sugar on the side and allow each person to put on his own brown sugar. No butter is even needed. The brown sugar melts as the sweet potato is mashed with a fork. A lot of people also like to add ground cinnamon.

6 to 8 medium sweet potatoes, washed

- Prick the potatoes with a fork.
- Wrap each potato individually in foil.
- Put the wrapped potatoes into a slow cooker.
- Cover and cook on high for 3 to 4½ hours or on low for 7 to 10 hours.

Yield: 6 to 8 servings

Calories: 130; Fat: 0g (0% fat); Cholesterol: 0mg; Carbohydrate: 33g; Dietary Fiber: 4g; Protein: 2g; Sodium: 45mg

 Menu idea: These potatoes complement any lean meat entrées— chicken, fish, or especially turkey.

Cabbage Casserole

Save time by letting the manufacturer do all the work. All you have to do is simply assemble and enjoy.

1 **(10-ounce) bag finely shredded cabbage (coleslaw)**	1 **(8-ounce) package lean diced ham**
1 **(8-ounce) bag fresh baby carrots**	2 **tablespoons Butter Buds Sprinkles**

- Spray a slow cooker with nonfat cooking spray.
- In the cooker stir together the cabbage, carrots, ham, and Sprinkles until well mixed.
- Cover and cook on high for 2 hours.

Yield: 4 (1-cup) servings

Calories: 124; Fat: 3g (22% fat); Cholesterol: 27mg; Carbohydrate: 12g; Dietary Fiber: 3g; Protein: 12g; Sodium: 1031mg

 Menu idea: This entrée tastes great with the Sweet Corn Bread Recipe (page 41), and because it's so low in calories you can have the Pinwheel Dinner Rolls from *Busy People's Low-Fat Cookbook* without feeling guilty.

Cheesy Potato and Broccoli Casserole

Now you can enjoy a cheesy casserole guilt free.

I	pound frozen fat-free shredded potatoes (hash browns)	I	(10 ³/₄-ounce) can fat-free broccoli cheese soup
I	(10-ounce) box frozen broccoli cuts	I	cup fat-free dairy creamer

- Spray a slow cooker with nonfat cooking spray.
- In the slow cooker mix together the potatoes, broccoli, soup, and creamer.
- Cover and cook on low for 6 to 7 hours.

Yield: 8 (¹/₂-cup) servings

Calories: 131; Fat: 1g (7% fat); Cholesterol: 3mg; Carbohydrate: 27g; Dietary Fiber: 3g; Protein: 3g; Sodium: 283mg

 Menu idea: These potatoes are especially good with a lean entrée, such as broiled or grilled fish or chicken breasts.

Cottage Potatoes

Watch out! These go fast.

1 (2-pound) package hash browns	1 (^{1}/2-ounce) envelope Butter Buds Mix, dry (or 2 tablespoons Ultra Promise)
1 (10^3/4-ounce) can 98% fat-free cream of chicken soup	
1 (8-ounce) package fat-free cheddar cheese	1 bunch green onions, chopped, tops and all
2 cups fat-free sour cream	1 red or green pepper, chopped (the red makes it more colorful)

- Spray a slow cooker with nonfat cooking spray.
- In the slow cooker mix together the hash browns, soup, cheese, sour cream, Butter Buds, onions, and pepper.
- Cover and cook on high until hot and bubbly, about 3 hours.

Yield: 16 (^{1}/2-cup) servings

Calories: 121; Fat: 0g (0% fat); Cholesterol: 3mg; Carbohydrate: 21g; Dietary Fiber: 2g; Protein: 8g; Sodium: 327mg

 Menu idea: This side dish is an excellent source of healthy carbohydrates and when served with the Green Bean Delight (page 108) along with a serving of lean protein such as baked, grilled, or broiled fish, turkey, chicken, or ham it makes a complete meal.

Green Beans & Potatoes

2	(15-ounce) cans green beans, drained	2	tablespoons fat-free buttery spread (I use Fleischmann's.)
3	cooked red potatoes, not peeled and cut into $\frac{1}{2}$-inch cubes	4	tablespoons bacon bits
		$\frac{1}{8}$	teaspoon garlic salt, optional
			Dash of pepper, optional

- Spray a slow cooker with nonfat cooking spray.
- In the cooker mix together the green beans, potatoes, butter spread, and bacon bits.
- Cover and cook on high for 2 to 3 hours or on low for 6 hours.
- Season with the garlic salt and pepper, if using.

Yield: 6 ($\frac{1}{2}$-cup) servings

Calories: 67; Fat: 1g (9% fat); Cholesterol: 0mg; Carbohydrate: 13g; Dietary Fiber: 3g; Protein: 4g; Sodium: 368mg

 Menu idea: Good with lean meat entrées such as Breaded Pork Tenderloin from *Busy People's Low-Fat Cookbook*.

Maple Yams

These yams are sweetly kissed with a taste of Vermont, known for its wonderful maple syrup.

1 **(40-ounce) can cut yams (in light syrup with syrup drained)**	**Sprinkles**
1 **tablespoon Butter Buds**	**¹/₄ cup light maple syrup**

- Spray a slow cooker with nonfat cooking spray.
- Put the yams into the slow cooker.
- Break up the yams with a fork.
- Add the Butter Buds and maple syrup.
- With a hand-held mixer on low speed, mix everything together for 1 minute or until the potatoes are mashed to desired consistency.
- Cover and cook on low for 6 hours.

Note: You can also make this as a pocket pouch (page 6).

Yield: 6 (½-cup) servings

Calories: 187; Fat: 0g (0% fat); Cholesterol: 0mg; Carbohydrate: 45g; Dietary Fiber: 5g; Protein: 2g; Sodium: 158mg

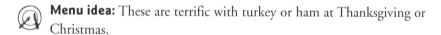 **Menu idea:** These are terrific with turkey or ham at Thanksgiving or Christmas.

Mashed Potatoes

Who'd ever think you could make mashed potatoes in the slow cooker, and without having to peel even one potato?

1¼ cups fat-free, refrigerated non-dairy creamer

¼ cup Butter Buds Sprinkles

1 pound frozen Southern-style hash browns (potatoes cut into tiny squares)

½ cup fat-free sour cream

4 ounces fat-free cream cheese

¾ cup skim milk

Salt and pepper, optional

- Spray a slow cooker with nonfat cooking spray.
- In the slow cooker mix together the non-dairy creamer with the Butter Buds Sprinkles until dissolved.
- Stir in the hash browns.
- Cover and cook on high for 2½ hours or on low for 4 to 5 hours.
- Unplug the cooker and add the sour cream, cream cheese, and milk.
- With a hand-held mixer beat all the ingredients together until thick and creamy.
- Cover and leave in the slow cooker to keep warm.
- If desired add the salt and pepper to taste.

Note: For fast and easy gravy, pour a can of your favorite gravy in a microwaveable container and heat in the microwave. Most cans and jars of gravy are low-fat (3g of fat per 100 calories) or fat-free.

Yield: 9 (½-cup) servings

Calories: 140; Fat: 0g (0% fat); Cholesterol: 1mg; Carbohydrate: 28g; Dietary Fiber: 1g; Protein: 5g; Sodium: 265mg

 Menu idea: Good with any lean meat, chicken, or fish entrée, along with a green vegetable.

Mashed Yams with an Orange Kiss

The orange juice with the pumpkin pie spice gives this dish an excellent flavor.

2 (40-ounce) cans yams, drained	1/2 cup fat-free margarine
4 ounces Egg Beaters	1/4 cup brown sugar
1/2 cup orange juice	1/2 teaspoon pumpkin pie spice

- Spray a slow cooker with nonfat cooking spray.
- Mash the yams in the slow cooker.
- Add the Egg Beaters, orange juice, margarine, brown sugar, and pumpkin spice and mix well with the mixer for about 1 minute.
- Cover and cook on low for 6 hours.

Yield: 14 (½-cup) servings

Calories: 189; Fat: 0g (0% fat); Cholesterol: 0mg; Carbohydrate: 43g; Dietary Fiber: 3g; Protein: 4g; Sodium: 191mg

 Menu idea: These are wonderful at Christmas and Thanksgiving.

Sweet Potato
Hawaiian-Style Casserole

Simply sensational.

1	(40-ounce) can yams, drained	2	tablespoons dark brown sugar
1	(10-ounce) can crushed pineapple, drained		

- Spray a slow cooker with nonfat cooking spray.
- Put the yams, pineapple, and brown sugar into the slow cooker.
- With a hand-held mixer on high speed beat all the ingredients together for 2 minutes, or until smooth and creamy.
- Cover and cook on low for 2 to 4 hours.

Yield: 8 (½-cup) servings

Calories: 176; Fat: 0g (0% fat); Cholesterol: 0mg; Carbohydrate: 41g; Dietary Fiber: 3g; Protein: 3g; Sodium: 111mg

 Menu idea: This casserole is a terrific complement to ham and lean cuts of pork.

Twice Baked Mashed Potatoes

If you like smooth and creamy, you'll like these potatoes.

1¼ cups refrigerated, fat-free non-dairy creamer	½ cup fat-free sour cream
¼ cup Butter Buds Sprinkles	4 ounces fat-free cream cheese
1 pound frozen Southern style hash browns (potatoes cut into tiny squares)	¾ cup skim milk
	½ cup real bacon bits
	¼ cup fresh chives
	Salt and pepper, optional

- Spray a slow cooker with nonfat cooking spray.
- In the cooker mix the non-dairy creamer with the Butter Buds Sprinkles until dissolved.
- Stir in the hash browns.
- Cover and cook on high for 2½ hours or on low for 4 to 5 hours.
- Unplug the cooker and add the sour cream, cream cheese, milk, bacon bits, and fresh chives.
- With a hand-held mixer beat all the ingredients together until thick and creamy.
- Cover and leave in the slow cooker to keep warm.
- If desired add the salt and pepper to taste.

Note: For fast and easy gravy, pour a can of your favorite gravy in a microwaveable container and heat in the microwave. Most cans and jars of gravy are low-fat (3g of fat per 100 calories) or fat-free.

Yield: 9 (½-cup) servings

Calories: 161; Fat: 1g (8% fat); Cholesterol: 6mg; Carbohydrate: 29g; Dietary Fiber: 1g; Protein: 7g; Sodium: 465mg

 Menu idea: These potatoes are good with any lean meat, chicken, or fish entrée, along with a green vegetable.

Minestrone Macaroni

Easy on your pocketbook and your waistline.

1 pound ground meatless burger or 1 pound pre-cooked ground eye of round beef	1 (16-ounce) can kidney beans, rinsed and drained
2 (14½-ounce) cans Italian diced tomatoes, not drained	1 (15-ounce) can garbanzo beans, rinsed and drained
2¼ cups low-sodium beef broth	1 (14½-ounce) can cut green beans, drained
1½ cups uncooked elbow macaroni	

- Spray a slow cooker with nonfat cooking spray.
- In the cooker mix together the meatless burger, tomatoes, and beef broth.
- Cover and cook on high for 1½ hours.
- Add the macaroni and cook until tender (15 to 20 minutes).
- Stir in all the beans and heat through.

Yield: 12 (1-cup) servings

Calories: 188; Fat: 1g (4% fat); Cholesterol: 0mg; Carbohydrate: 30g; Dietary Fiber: 7g; Protein: 15g; Sodium: 557mg

 Menu idea: This is very good with tabbouleh salad. You can garnish the top of each bowl with shredded fat-free cheddar cheese. I served this with a green salad and garlic breadsticks.

Sweetened Carrots

It doesn't get any easier than this—simple and good.

¹/₂ cup water	**2 pounds fresh baby carrots**
¹/₄ cup sugar	

- In a slow cooker stir together the water and sugar until the sugar is dissolved.
- Add the carrots.
- Cover and cook on low for 3 to 4 hours or until tender.
- Discard the water.
- Serve hot.

Note: You can also make this as a pocket pouch (page 6).

Yield: 6 (¹/₃-pound) servings

Calories: 90; Fat: 1g (8% fat); Cholesterol: 0mg; Carbohydrate: 21g; Dietary Fiber: 3g; Protein: 1g; Sodium: 53mg

 Menu idea: This goes great with home-style casseroles such as the Farmer's Casserole from *Busy People's Low-Fat Cookbook.*

Calico Beans

I converted a high-fat, higher-calorie recipe with many more ingredients to this tasty side dish. It's a terrific substitute for plain ol' baked beans. I'd be surprised if you ever go back to ol' baked beans again.

I (3-ounce) jar real bacon bits	I (15½-ounce) can dark red kidney beans, drained
½ cup frozen chopped onion	
½ cup ketchup	I (15-ounce) can large lima beans or butter beans, drained
I (16-ounce) can baked beans, not drained but with chunks of fatty bacon removed	½ cup no-calorie sweetener (I use Splenda, the box that says, "measures like sugar.")

- Spray a slow cooker with nonfat cooking spray.
- In the slow cooker mix together the bacon pieces, onion, ketchup, baked beans, kidney beans, lima beans, and sweetener.
- Cover and cook on high for 2 to 2½ hours or on low for 5 to 7 hours.

Yield: 9 (½-cup) servings

Calories: 170; Fat: 2g (10% fat); Cholesterol: 6mg; Carbohydrate: 28g; Dietary Fiber: 7g; Protein: 11g; Sodium: 926mg

 Menu idea: These beans are great for picnic potlucks.

Bacon Green Beans

A delicious blend of lightly sweetened beans with a touch of tartness.

2 (1-pound) bags frozen cut green beans	¹/₄ cup fat-free red wine vinegar salad dressing
¹/₃ cup teriyaki baste and glaze (I use Kikkoman.)	1 (3-ounce) jar real bacon bits
	1 cup chopped onion (frozen chopped onions are fine)

- Spray a slow cooker with nonfat cooking spray.
- In the slow cooker mix together the green beans, teriyaki, salad dressing, bacon bits, and onion.
- Cover and cook on high for 3½ to 4 hours or on low for 7 to 8 hours.

Note: You can also cut this recipe in half and make as a pocket pouch (page 6).

Yield: 12 (²/₃-cup) servings

Calories: 68; Fat: 1g (19% fat); Cholesterol: 5mg; Carbohydrate: 10g; Dietary Fiber: 2g; Protein: 4g; Sodium: 476mg

 Menu idea: A lean source of protein such as Orange Roughy or Smothered Steak, both from *Busy People's Low-Fat Cookbook*, complement this side dish.

"B.B.B." (Best Baked Beans)

My daughters loved these so much that they named the recipe themselves. They are very filling, satisfying, and delicious. No one would ever believe they're fat-free. Eat as a meal or side dish. A fun way to serve these as the entrée is in a pie pan as the plate and red handkerchiefs as napkins.

l	(l-pound) package ground meatless burger crumbles or l pound cooked ground eye of round beef (I use Morningstar Farms.)	2	(16-ounce) cans fat-free vegetarian baked beans
l	(15-ounce) can butter beans, drained	$^3/_4$	cup brown-sugar-flavored barbecue sauce
		$^1/_2$	cup chopped onion (for faster preparation use chopped frozen onions)

- Spray a slow cooker with nonfat cooking spray.
- In the cooker stir together the meatless burger, butter beans, baked beans, barbecue sauce, and onion until well mixed.
- Cover and cook on low for 4 to 5 hours.

Note: For those of you who don't like vegetarian meat substitute, you'll love this. In regards to the rest of the family, don't tell them it's not real beef and they'll *never* know. (Some things are better left unsaid.)

Yield: 16 ($^1/_2$-cup) servings

Calories: 124; Fat: 0g (0% fat); Cholesterol: 0mg; Carbohydrate: 20g; Dietary Fiber: 5g; Protein: 12g; Sodium: 584mg (Based on using ground meatless burger. Add 1.56g fat for eye of round.)

 Menu idea: These beans are good with a vegetable tray and a fresh fruit salad for a lunch or as a complement to any meat.

Buttered Collard Greens with Ham

A southern favorite.

4 (15-ounce) cans chopped collard greens	1 pound boiled ham, thinly sliced and cut into bite-size pieces
2 apples, quartered, with seeds removed	1 medium onion, chopped (approximately 1 cup)
2 tablespoons Butter Buds Sprinkles	

- Spray a slow cooker with nonfat cooking spray.
- Drain the collard greens.
- In the cooker mix together the greens, apples, Butter Buds, ham, and onion.
- Cover and cook on high for 2 to 3 hours or on low for 4 to 6 hours.

Yield: 12 (½-cup) servings

Calories: 85; Fat: 2g (18% fat); Cholesterol: 36mg; Carbohydrate: 11g; Dietary Fiber: 4g; Protein: 9g; Sodium: 542mg

 Menu idea: In another slow cooker cook Cottage Potatoes (page 92) and serve with chilled watermelon slices.

Creamed Green Beans & Ham

A heartland favorite.

4	(15-ounce) cans green beans, drained	1	(12-ounce) can fat-free evaporated skim milk
1/2	pound extra lean ham, chopped	1	tablespoon Butter Buds Sprinkles
1	(8-ounce) can mushroom stems and pieces, drained, optional	2	tablespoons cornstarch

- Spray a slow cooker with nonfat cooking spray.
- In the slow cooker mix together the green beans, ham, mushrooms, evaporated milk, Butter Buds, and cornstarch.
- Cover and cook for 5 hours on low.
- Serve hot.

Yield: 12 (½-cup) servings

Calories: 76; Fat: 1g (12% fat); Cholesterol: 7mg; Carbohydrate: 10g; Dietary Fiber: 2g; Protein: 7g; Sodium: 562mg

 Menu idea: As a fabulous source of carbohydrates this side dish is wonderful served with lean proteins such as Smothered Steak or my homemade Chicken Nuggets, both from *Busy People's Low-Fat Cookbook.*

Garlic Beans

If you like Boston Market's green beans, you'll love these.

1 **pound frozen green beans**	**Light salt**
4 **ounces sliced fresh mushrooms**	**Pepper**
1/4 **cup Butter Buds Sprinkles, dry**	1/2 **cup fat-free chicken or beef**
1 **tablespoon minced garlic (I use the kind in a jar.)**	**broth (made from bouillon is fine)**

- Spray a slow cooker with nonfat cooking spray.
- In the slow cooker mix together the green beans, mushrooms, Butter Buds, garlic, and salt and pepper to taste.
- Add the broth.
- Cover and cook on high for 3 hours or on low for 6 hours.

Note: You can also make this as a pocket pouch (page 6).

Yield: 8 (½-cup) servings

Calories: 33; Fat: 0g (0% fat); Cholesterol: 0mg; Carbohydrate: 8g; Dietary Fiber: 2g; Protein: 2g; Sodium: 211mg

 Menu idea: Great side dish for any home-style meal such as Manhandler Meatloaf from *Busy People's Low-Fat Cookbook.*

Glazed Green Beans

I'm often asked, "What is your secret ingredient? They taste so good."

1 (3-ounce) jar real bacon bits	1/2 cup teriyaki baste and glaze (I use Kikkoman.)
1 large onion cut into 1/4-inch slices	1/4 cup water
2 (16-ounce) bags frozen cut green beans	1/2 teaspoon garlic salt

- Spray a slow cooker with nonfat cooking spray.
- In the slow cooker mix together the bacon bits, onion, green beans, teriyaki glaze, water, and garlic salt.
- Cover and cook on high for 3 to 4 hours or on low for 8 to 10 hours.
- Serve hot.

Note: Keeps well in the slow cooker on low. Reheats well in the microwave.

Note: You can also cut the recipe in half and make it as a pocket pouch (page 6).

Yield: 12 (⅔-cup) servings

Calories: 72; Fat: 1g (17% fat); Cholesterol: 5mg; Carbohydrate: 11g; Dietary Fiber: 2g; Protein: 5g; Sodium: 575 mg

 Menu idea: Great for potlucks, buffets, and as a holiday side dish with ham, turkey, or beef.

Green Bean Delight

This is one of my favorite ways to prepare green beans.

1 medium onion, chopped	3 (15½-ounce) cans French-style
8 ounces mushrooms, thinly	green beans, drained
sliced	3 tablespoons honey
½ cup liquid Butter Buds	1 teaspoon light salt, optional
8 ounces lean ham, diced	

- Spray a slow cooker with nonfat cooking spray.
- In the slow cooker mix together the onion, mushrooms, Butter Buds, ham, green beans, honey, and salt, if using.
- Cover and cook on high 2 hours or on low for 4 to 8 hours.

Note: You can also make this as a pocket pouch (page 6).

Yield: 15 (½-cup) servings

Calories: 56; Fat: 1g (12% fat); Cholesterol: 5mg; Carbohydrate: 9g; Dietary Fiber: 2g; Protein: 5g; Sodium: 376mg

 Menu idea: Serve these with any home-style entrée such as Swiss Steak & Potatoes from *Busy People's Low-Fat Cookbook.*

Hawaiian-Style Baked Beans

A delicious twist to an old-time favorite, which is packed with protein.

2	(16-ounce) cans vegetarian baked beans	4	ounces extra lean cooked ham, cut into bite-size pieces
¼	cup chopped onion (for faster preparation use frozen chopped onions)	1	(8-ounce) can crushed pineapple in unsweetened pineapple juice, drained
¼	cup Kikkoman's Teriyaki Baste & Glaze		

- Spray a slow cooker with nonfat cooking spray.
- In the cooker stir the beans, onion, Baste & Glaze, ham, and pineapple and stir until well mixed.
- Cover and cook on low for 4 hours.

Yield: 11 (½-cup) servings

Calories: 112; Fat: 1g (7% fat); Cholesterol: 5mg; Carbohydrate: 22g; Dietary Fiber: 4g; Protein: 6g; Sodium: 622mg

 Menu idea: These beans are always a favorite at picnic potlucks. I serve them with fresh wedges of watermelon and crunchy vegetable sticks along with my Vegetable Dip from *Busy People's Low-Fat Cookbook*.

Mama's Beans

These tender green beans are made with convenient ingredients you probably already have on hand.

1 **(16-ounce) bag frozen cut green beans**	1 **tablespoon grated Parmesan cheese**
4 **slices hardwood-smoked, white turkey lunchmeat, cut into tiny pieces**	**Dash of pepper, optional**
	1 **teaspoon fat-free garlic butter sprinkles, optional (I use Molly McButter.)**

- Spray a slow cooker with nonfat cooking spray.
- In the slow cooker mix together the green beans, turkey, and Parmesan cheese.
- Add the pepper and garlic butter, if desired.
- Cover and cook on high for 3 hours or on low for 7 to 9 hours. The dish is completely cooked when the beans are hot.
- Serve as a side dish or eat as a main meal.

Note: You can also make this as a pocket pouch (page 6).

Yield: 4 ($\frac{1}{2}$-cup) servings

Calories: 57; Fat: 1g (13% fat); Cholesterol: 6mg; Carbohydrate: 9g; Dietary Fiber: 3g; Protein: 5g; Sodium: 155mg

Menu idea: This is one of my all-time fast and easy favorite holiday side dishes to prepare. It tastes exceptionally delicious with pork tenderloin or turkey or lean ham.

Pineapple Baked Beans

Great for a potluck. Everyone will want the recipe.

1	pound ground meatless burger (I use Morningstar Farms.)	1 cup mild chunky salsa
1	(28-ounce) can baked beans	1/2 cup barbecue sauce
1	(8-ounce) can sugar-free pineapple tidbits, drained	1 teaspoon minced garlic

- Spray a slow cooker with nonfat cooking spray.
- In the cooker stir together the ground meatless, baked beans, pineapple, salsa, barbecue sauce, and garlic until well mixed.
- Cover and cook on low for 4 to 8 hours until bubbly.

Yield: 15 (1/2-cup) servings

Calories: 108; Fat: 0g (0% fat); Cholesterol: 0mg; Carbohydrate: 17g; Dietary Fiber: 5g; Protein: 9g; Sodium: 487mg

 Menu idea: These beans are great with a fresh vegetable tray and fat-free Vegetable Dip in *Busy People's Fat-Free Cookbook*.

Spiced Apples

These are so good, even thinking about them makes my mouth water.

4	Jonathan apples, peeled, cored, and sliced into $1/4$-inch slices	1	teaspoon ground cinnamon
2	tablespoons Butter Buds Sprinkles	$1/4$	cup dark brown sugar
		2	tablespoons water

- Spray a slow cooker with nonfat cooking spray.
- In the slow cooker mix together the apples, Butter Buds, cinnamon, brown sugar, and water.
- Cover and cook on high for $3\frac{1}{2}$ to $4\frac{1}{2}$ hours or on low for 7 to 9 hours.

Note: You can also make this as a pocket pouch (page 6).

Yield: 4 servings

Calories: 142; Fat: 1g (3% fat); Cholesterol: 0mg; Carbohydrate: 38g; Dietary Fiber: 4g; Protein: 0g; Sodium: 118mg

 Menu idea: The pineapple in this recipe complements pork tenderloin and lean ham. Side dishes that taste great with this are Pineapple Fluff or Tropical Passion Fruit Salad, both from *Busy People's Low-Fat Cookbook.*

Sweet Peas & Pearl Onions

A fast and unique way to assemble this recipe without a lot of fuss.

I	(15-ounce) jar pearl onions, drained	2	(15-ounce) cans sweet peas, drained
		3	tablespoons honey

- Spray a slow cooker with nonfat cooking spray.
- In the slow cooker gently stir together the onions, peas, and honey.
- Cover and cook on low for 8 hours.
- Serve hot.

Note: You can also make this as a pocket pouch (page 6).

Yield: 7 ($\frac{1}{2}$-cup) servings

Calories: 135; Fat: 0g (0% fat); Cholesterol: 0mg; Carbohydrate: 28g; Dietary Fiber: 4g; Protein: 5g; Sodium: 332mg

 Menu idea: This vegetable recipe is great with any lean meat.

Calico Corn

The colorful combination of this side dish brightens any meal. The flavor combination does, too.

2 (15¼-ounce) cans whole kernel corn, drained	¼ cup fat-free French dressing
1 tablespoon sugar	1 cup chunky salsa, your favorite

- Spray a slow cooker with nonfat cooking spray.
- In the slow cooker mix together the corn, sugar, dressing, and salsa.
- Cover and cook on low for 3 hours.

Note: You can also make this as a pocket pouch (page 6).

Yield: 7 (½-cup) servings

Calories: 108; Fat: 1g (8% fat); Cholesterol: 0mg; Carbohydrate: 24g; Dietary Fiber: 2g; Protein: 3g; Sodium: 454mg

 Menu idea: This corn is great for a fish fry and complements just about any meal.

Corn on the Cob

Yes, you can *cook corn on the cob in your slow cooker. It is so easy.*

6 to 8 ears of corn

- Place the corn into a slow cooker. Do not use big, long ears of corn, because they won't fit in your slow cooker.
- Fill the cooker three-fourths full with hot water.
- Cover and cook on low for 3 to 4 hours. The husk and silk of the ears of corn will come off easily after they are cooked. Simply wear potholder mittens when husking the corn.

Yield: 6 to 8 (1-ear) servings

Calories: 68; Fat: 1g (10% fat); Cholesterol: 0mg; Carbohydrate: 15g; Dietary Fiber: 3g; Protein: 3g; Sodium: 0mg

Menu idea: Great for cookouts, picnics, and camping. Because corn is high in calories and carbohydrates, I encourage eating it with proteins lower in calories, such as broiled or grilled fish or chicken breast.

Zesty Corn

This will add zest to any boring meal.

1 (16-ounce) can cream-style yellow corn	1 cup chunky salsa
1 (16-ounce) can white (or yellow) corn, drained	

- Spray a slow cooker with nonfat cooking spray.
- In the slow cooker mix together the cream corn, corn, and salsa.
- Cover and cook on low for 2 to 3 hours.

Note: You can also make this as a pocket pouch (page 6).

Yield: 8 (1/2-cup) servings

Calories: 85; Fat: 1g (7% fat); Cholesterol: 0mg; Carbohydrate: 19g; Dietary Fiber: 2g; Protein: 2g; Sodium: 439mg

 Menu idea: This corn is fantastic with grilled fish or chicken.

Entrées

You can tell how big a person is by what it takes to discourage him.

Barbecue Chicken
with Corn on the Cob

It's every bit as good as you'd hoped it would be.

2	pounds boneless, skinless chicken breasts	1	(6-mini-ear) package frozen corn on the cob or 3 whole ears of corn, husked and cut in half
1	(16- to 18-ounce) bottle barbecue sauce		

- Spray a slow cooker with nonfat cooking spray.
- Place the chicken breasts in the cooker.
- Pour the barbecue sauce over the chicken.
- Put all the mini ears of corn in foil and wrap to seal.
- Place the foil-wrapped ears on top of the barbecued chicken.
- Cover and cook on low for 7 to 8 hours.

Yield: 6 servings (5 ounces chicken and 1 mini ear of corn on the cob)

Calories: 262; Fat: 4g (13% fat); Cholesterol: 88mg; Carbohydrate: 18g; Dietary Fiber: 2g; Protein: 38g; Sodium: 721mg

 Menu idea: You can enjoy a picnic even in the winter by adding some all-time favorites like Sassy Slaw and Brownie Cookies, both from *Busy People's Low-Fat Cookbook*.

Beanie Baby Stew

This is a breeze to put together and a crowd pleaser every time.

1 **(24-ounce) can deluxe Great Northern beans**	1 **(7-ounce) can diced green chiles**
2 **(10-ounce) cans white chicken chunks in water, drained**	1 **pound frozen diced potatoes (the kind used for hash browns)**
1 **(49 1/2-ounce) can fat-free chicken broth**	1/2 **cup cornstarch**
1 **(12-ounce) bag frozen chopped onions**	**Fat-free mozzarella cheese, for garnish**

- Spray a slow cooker with nonfat cooking spray.
- In the slow cooker stir together the beans, chicken, chicken broth, onions, chiles, and potatoes until well mixed.
- Cover and cook on high for 4 hours or on low for 8 to 9 hours.
- With a ladle or strainer remove as much of the cooked ingredients as possible and put them into a large bowl.
- With a potato masher smash the cooked food for about 1 minute. (This will make the broth thicker.)
- Combine the cornstarch with 1/2 cup cold water. Stir briskly until the cornstarch is completely dissolved.
- Stir the dissolved cornstarch into the broth in the slow cooker until well mixed.
- Return the cooked vegetables (previously smashed) to the cooker and stir.
- Turn to high, cover, and cook for another 20 to 30 minutes. The stew will be thick and creamy when done.
- If desired, sprinkle each serving bowl of stew lightly with fat-free mozzarella cheese just before eating.

Yield: 14 (1-cup) servings

Calories: 171; Fat: 3g (18% fat); Cholesterol: 25mg; Carbohydrate: 21g; Dietary Fiber: 6g; Protein: 14g; Sodium: 715 mg

 Menu idea: This is good with a fresh vegetable tray and fat-free saltine crackers.

Chicken à la King

This very tasty dish is creatively made. By allowing pasta to sit with the other ingredients overnight, it becomes a thick, creamy base for our Chicken a la King.

1 (12 1/2-ounce) can chicken breast in water, not drained	1 (10 3/4-ounce) can 98 percent fat-free cream of mushroom condensed soup—Do not make as directed.
1 (15-ounce) can sweet peas	
1 (7 1/4-ounce) box macaroni and cheese (Use pasta only.) Do not make as directed.	1 cup refrigerated fat-free non-dairy creamer
1 1/2 cups hot water	1/4 cup chopped pimiento, optional

- Spray a slow cooker with nonfat cooking spray.
- In the cooker gently stir together the chicken breast with its water, sweet peas, macaroni, hot water, and mushroom soup.
- Cover and place the entire slow cooker in the refrigerator for 8 to 12 hours or overnight.
- Remove the cooker from refrigeration.
- Cook on high for 2½ to 3 hours.
- Gently stir for 2 to 4 minutes or until pasta dissolves and gets thick and creamy.
- Gently stir in the creamer until well blended. Stir in the chopped pimiento, if using.
- Serve over toast or baked biscuits.

Yield: 14 (½-cup) servings

Calories: 122; Fat: 1g (9% fat); Cholesterol: 12mg; Carbohydrate: 18g; Dietary Fiber: 1g; Protein: 7g; Sodium: 313mg

★ **Cheesy Chicken à la King:** Stir in the cheese packet from the box of macaroni and cheese when stirring all the ingredients together.

Calories: 132; Fat: 1g (11% fat); Cholesterol: 14mg; Carbohydrate: 19g; Dietary Fiber: 1g; Protein: 8g; Sodium: 430mg

 Menu idea: Serve this dish with your favorite green vegetable on the side.

Chicken & Angel Hair Pasta

All your little angels will like this.

1 pound boneless, skinless chicken breasts, cut into bite-size cubes	8 ounces fresh sliced mushrooms
1 (1¹/₅-ounce) envelope onion soup mix, dry	1 (8-ounce) package fat-free sour cream
3 cups water	2 tablespoons fresh chopped chives, optional
1 tablespoon minced garlic	8 ounces uncooked Mueller's brand angel hair pasta

- Spray a slow cooker with nonfat cooking spray.
- In the cooker mix the chicken, onion soup mix, water, garlic, mushrooms, sour cream, and chives, if using.
- Cover and cook on high for 3 hours. Add the pasta the last 10 minutes of cooking.

Yield: 6 (1-cup) servings

Calories: 293; Fat: 2g (6% fat); Cholesterol: 44mg; Carbohydrate: 40g; Dietary Fiber: 2g; Protein: 27g; Sodium: 591mg

 Menu idea: For a meal everyone will enjoy serve this with the Green Bean Pocket Pouch (page 8) along with Peaches and Cream Gelatin Salad from *Busy People's Low-Fat Cookbook.*

Chicken & Pasta Casserole

Two thumbs up for this winning chicken casserole.

1½ cups uncooked Mueller's brand elbow macaroni	1 (8½-ounce) can sweet peas and carrot combination, drained
1 (14½-ounce) can fat-free chicken broth	1 (4-ounce) can mushroom stems and pieces, drained
1 (12½-ounce) can fat-free chicken breast, not drained	4 tablespoons grated Parmesan cheese

- Spray a slow cooker with nonfat cooking spray.
- Turn the cooker on high. In the cooker gently stir together the macaroni, chicken broth, and chicken. Try not to break up the chicken.
- Cover and cook on high for 1½ hours or until the macaroni is cooked, but not over-cooked.
- Stir in the peas and carrots and mushrooms.
- Cover and unplug the slow cooker. Let it sit for 10 minutes. The heat from the dish will heat up the vegetables.
- Put a 1-cup serving on each plate, and sprinkle each serving with 2 teaspoons of grated Parmesan cheese.

Yield: 6 (1-cup) servings

Calories: 200; Fat: 3g (13% fat); Cholesterol: 28mg; Carbohydrate: 23g; Dietary Fiber: 1g; Protein: 18g; Sodium: 585mg

 Menu idea: This is a complete entrée. Serve it with a tossed salad.

Chicken and Potato Stew

This smooth and comforting stew helps bring relaxation to even the most hectic days.

I	pound boneless, skinless chicken breasts cut into bite-size pieces	2	(16-ounce) packages frozen vegetables for stew
I	(10³/₄-ounce) can 98% fat-free cream of mushroom soup	2	tablespoons fat-free butter

- Spray a slow cooker with nonfat cooking spray.
- Layer in the cooker in the following order the chicken, soup, frozen vegetables, and butter.
- Cook on low for 7 to 9 hours.

Yield: 6 (1-cup) servings

Calories: 199; Fat: 1g (6% fat); Cholesterol: 44mg; Carbohydrate: 24g; Dietary; Fiber: 1g; Protein: 20g; Sodium: 289mg

Menu idea: This stew is great with the Spiced Apples Pocket Pouch (page 9).

Chicken Dumpling Casserole

I was so happy when I figured out how to cook noodles in the slow cooker. You'll be pleased, too.

3	cups hot water	3	(12-ounce) jars fat-free chicken gravy
8	ounces fat-free shredded cheddar cheese	1	(16-ounce) can mixed vegetables, drained
1	(4-ounce) jar mushrooms, drained	1	(12-ounce) bag eggless dumplings (Use only No-Yolk.)
2	(10-ounce) cans chicken breast		

- Spray a slow cooker with nonfat cooking spray.
- In the slow cooker mix together the water, cheese, mushrooms, chicken breast, gravy, and vegetables.
- Add the Spiced Apples Pocket Pouch at this time if you are making them with this entrée.
- Cover and cook on low for 8 hours.
- If making the Spiced Apples, remove them from the slow cooker.
- Turn to high, cover, and cook for 5 minutes.
- Stir in the dumplings, making sure dumplings are completely covered with liquid.
- Continue cooking for ½ hour more or until the dumplings are tender.

Note: If some of the dumplings accidentally rise above the liquid and become dry, simply remove those few dumplings with a slotted spoon before serving.

Yield: 12 (1-cup) servings

Calories: 228; Fat: 1g (5% fat); Cholesterol: 22mg; Carbohydrate: 32g; Dietary Fiber: 3g; Protein: 20g; Sodium: 843mg

 Menu idea: Spiced Apples Pocket Pouch (page 9) complements this casserole. A 6-quart or larger slow cooker is needed if you are making the Spiced Apples.

Chicken Chili

This reminds me of a cross between bean soup and chili, but made with chicken. Definitely a winner.

1	(48-ounce) jar deluxe Great Northern beans	1/2	cup frozen chopped onion
1	(4-ounce) can diced green chiles	1 1/2	teaspoon chili powder
2	(10-ounce) cans chicken breast, not drained	1	cup fat-free chicken broth
		9	tablespoons fat-free sour cream (1 tablespoon per 1 cup serving)

- Spray a slow cooker with nonfat cooking spray.
- In the cooker stir together the Great Northern beans, green chiles, chicken breast, onion, chili powder, and chicken broth until well mixed.
- Cover and cook on high for 3 to 4 hours or on low for 6 to 9 hours.
- Stir 1 tablespoon fat-free sour cream into each 1-cup serving.

Yield: 9 (1-cup) servings

Calories: 223; Fat: 2g (8% fat); Cholesterol: 27mg; Carbohydrate: 28g; Dietary Fiber: 13g; Protein: 21g; Sodium: 894mg

 Menu idea: You'll get rave reviews when you serve this chili with the Parmesan Garlic Quick Bread (page 38).

Chicken Cobbler

This is country cooking at its best.

1 pound boneless, skinless chicken breasts, cut into bite-size pieces	1/2 cup frozen chopped onion (or 1 medium onion, chopped)
1 (1-pound) package frozen mixed vegetables (peas, corn, carrots, green beans, and lima beans)	2 (12-ounce) jars fat-free chicken gravy
	1 1/2 cups dry pancake mix
	3/4 cup fat-free, low-sodium chicken broth

- Spray a slow cooker with nonfat cooking spray.
- In the cooker stir together the chicken, frozen vegetables, onion, and gravy until well mixed.
- Cover and cook on high for 2 hours.
- In a medium bowl stir the pancake mix and broth together to make a thick batter.
- Spread the batter over the boiling gravy in the slow cooker.
- Cover and cook on high for another 1/2 hour.

Yield: 5 servings

Calories: 315; Fat: 2g (4% fat); Cholesterol: 53mg; Carbohydrate: 49g; Dietary Fiber: 7g; Protein: 29g; Sodium: 1137mg

★ **Pork Cobbler:** Substitute pork tenderloin for the chicken and fat-free pork gravy for the chicken gravy.

Calories: 324; Fat: 4g (9% fat); Cholesterol: 59mg; Carbohydrate: 49g; Dietary Fiber: 7g; Protein: 27g; Sodium: 1123mg

★ **Beef Cobbler:** Substitute beef tenderloin for the chicken and fat-free beef gravy.

Calories: 356; Fat: 7g (17% fat); Cholesterol: 56mg; Carbohydrate: 49g; Dietary Fiber: 7g; Protein: 27g; Sodium: 1120mg

 Menu idea: For a complete meal serve this with Tangy Tossed Salad and Spiced Cookies, both from *Busy People's Low-Fat Cookbook*.

Chicken-N-Spaghetti

When making spaghetti make extra noodles and keep them in water in the refrigerator for up to three days before making this meal. Simply drain the water and your pasta is ready for this family-favorite meal.

1	(12-ounce) can fat-free chicken-flavored gravy	2	cups leftover chicken breast (approximately 1 pound), cut into chunks
2	cups cooked spaghetti (Use only Mueller's brand.)		

- Spray a slow cooker with nonfat cooking spray.
- Mix together the gravy with the cooked pasta and chicken in a slow cooker.
- Cover and cook on low for 2½ hours.

*Note: Leftover spaghetti noodles will work if you have them. Just soak the cooked spaghetti completely in a bowl of water in the refrigerator until you need them for this recipe.

Yield: 4 (1-cup) servings

Calories: 238; Fat: 3g (12% fat); Cholesterol: 59mg; Carbohydrate: 24g; Dietary Fiber: 1g; Protein: 27g; Sodium: 533mg

 Menu idea: This is good served with a broccoli pocket pouch and sugar-free Jell-O with mandarin oranges in it.

Chicken Enchilada Casserole

Slightly spicy and oh, so good.

2 (10-ounce) cans mild enchilada sauce	1 (8-ounce) bag fat-free shredded cheddar cheese
2 (10-ounce) cans chicken breast in water, drained	1 (11-ounce) package fat-free tortillas
1 cup fat-free sour cream	

- Spray a slow cooker with nonfat cooking spray.
- In a large bowl mix the enchilada sauce, chicken, and sour cream together until all of the chunks of chicken are shredded and the sauce is well blended.
- Place one-fourth of each of the following in layers in the slow cooker: sauce, cheese, and tortillas. Some of the tortillas have to be torn in order to fill in the gaps between the whole tortillas and the edge of the slow cooker. End with the sauce on top.
- Cover and cook on low for 2 to 2½ hours. This recipe does not do well cooked on high.
- Cut the casserole into six pieces.

Yield: 6 servings

Calories: 369; Fat: 4g (12% fat); Cholesterol: 44mg; Carbohydrate: 41g; Dietary Fiber: 2g; Protein: 35g; Sodium: 1351mg

★ **Beef Enchilada Casserole:** Substitute 1½ pounds precooked, lean, shredded eye of round beef for the chicken.

Calories: 461; Fat: 8g (17% fat); Cholesterol: 82mg; Carbohydrate: 41g; Dietary Fiber: 2g; Protein: 50g; Sodium: 1053mg

 Menu idea: For a fun meal with a southwestern theme start with Taco Soup from *Busy People's Low-Fat Cookbook* and a side salad of shredded lettuce, chopped tomatoes, salsa, crushed tortilla chips, and your favorite fat-free ranch dressing.

Chicken Stroganoff

Pasta lovers love this.

1	pound chicken breasts, cut into ¹/₂-inch cubes	2	teaspoons minced garlic
¹/₂	pound frozen chopped onions	3	cups chicken broth
1	(4-ounce) can mushroom stems and pieces, not drained	4	cups medium, No-Yolk brand egg noodles
		1	cup fat-free sour cream

- Spray a slow cooker with nonfat cooking spray.
- In the cooker stir the chicken, onions, mushrooms, garlic, and chicken broth together until well mixed.
- Cover and cook on low for 4 to 6 hours or on high for 2 to 3 hours. If cooking on low, turn the temperature to high before stirring in the noodles.
- Stir in the noodles, cover, and cook for another 30 minutes or until the noodles are cooked.
- Stir in the sour cream and serve.

Yield: 7 (1-cup) servings

Calories: 357; Fat: 1g (4% fat); Cholesterol: 38mg; Carbohydrate: 55g; Dietary Fiber: 3g; Protein: 26g; Sodium: 357mg

 Menu idea: For a meal your family will want again and again serve this recipe with Spiced Apples (page 112) and Broccoli Parmesan in *Busy People's Low-Fat Cookbook.*

Chicken Open-Faced Sandwiches with Gravy and Mashed Potatoes

This is an old country favorite.

2	(15-ounce) cans whole potatoes, not drained	1/2	cup skim milk
1	pound boneless, skinless chicken breasts, cooked and cut thinly	2	ounces fat-free cream cheese
2	(12-ounce) jars fat-free chicken-flavored gravy	1	tablespoon reduced-fat margarine
		5	slices fat-free white bread

- Put both cans of potatoes in the bottom of a slow cooker.
- Make a bowl out of heavy-duty (18-inch-wide) aluminum foil by pressing the foil into the slow cooker. Let the bottom of the foil bowl rest on top of the potatoes. Fold the remaining foil over the edge of the cooker and let the extra foil overhang on the outside of the slow cooker.
- Gently stir together the chicken and gravy in the foil bowl.
- Cover and cook on low for 3 hours.
- Remove the foil bowl of chicken and gravy.
- Drain the water from the potatoes.
- In the slow cooker add to the potatoes the milk, cream cheese, and margarine. Break up the potatoes. With the mixer on medium speed beat together all of the ingredients in the slow cooker to make mashed potatoes. If desired more milk can be added.
- Set out five dinner plates. On each plate place 1 slice of bread. Put 1 cup of the meat and gravy on the bread and 1/2 cup of the mashed potatoes next to it. Serve immediately.

Yield: 5 servings (1 cup gravy, 1/2 cup mashed potatoes, and 1 slice bread per serving)

Calories: 304; Fat: 3g (8% fat); Cholesterol: 55mg; Carbohydrate: 38g; Dietary Fiber: 3g; Protein: 29g; Sodium: 1428mg

 Menu idea: For a well-balanced meal simply serve with one of your favorite green vegetables such as steamed green beans or cooked spinach.

Chicken Holiday Barbecue

This is too good to limit serving only for the holidays.

1	(16-ounce) can jellied cranberry sauce	2	pounds boneless, skinless chicken breast
1	cup honey-mustard barbecue sauce	8	medium-size potatoes

- Spray a slow cooker with nonfat cooking spray.
- In the slow cooker mix together the cranberry sauce and barbecue sauce until well blended.
- With a knife make little cuts, about ½-inch deep, around the outside of the chicken. Place the chicken in the cooker and cover with the sauce.
- Place the potatoes on top of the chicken.
- Cook on low for 8 to 9 hours or on high for 4 hours.

Note: If desired, in order for the meat to absorb more flavor, put your meat and sauce in a Ziploc bag a few days ahead of time to marinate.

Yield: 8 servings (4 ounces chicken and 1 potato)

Calories: 356; Fat: 1g (3% fat); Cholesterol: 66mg; Carbohydrate: 60g; Dietary Fiber: 4g; Protein: 30g; Sodium: 406mg

★ **Ham Holiday Barbecue:** Substitute 2 pounds extra lean ham for the chicken.

Calories: 385; Fat: 6g (12% fat); Cholesterol: 34mg; Carbohydrate: 61g; Dietary Fiber: 4g; Protein: 28g; Sodium: 1619mg

★ **Pork Holiday Barbecue:** Substitute 2 pounds pork tenderloin for the chicken.

Calories: 367; Fat: 4g (9% fat); Cholesterol: 74mg; Carbohydrate: 60g; Dietary Fiber: 4g; Protein: 28g; Sodium: 389mg

 Menu idea: Once the meal is completely cooked, cut the potatoes in half. Spoon the sauce over the potatoes and meat when serving. Serve with steamed asparagus and fresh rolls.

Chicken Roll-Ups

2 cups boiling water	1 (16-ounce) package roasted chicken breast lunchmeat slices
1 (1/2-ounce) package Butter Buds Sprinkles, or 1 tablespoon Butter Buds Mix	1 (12-ounce) jar chicken-flavored gravy, your favorite
3/4 cup chopped mushrooms	
1 (6-serving-size) box chicken-flavored stuffing mix	

- Spray a slow cooker with nonfat cooking spray.
- In a medium-size covered bowl pour the boiling water and stir in the Butter Buds, mushrooms, stuffing mix (including the seasoning packet) and mix together.
- Cover tightly and let stand for 5 minutes.
- Press 2 tablespoons of stuffing in the middle of each slice of lunchmeat.
- Bring the sides of the lunchmeat into the middle and secure with a toothpick.
- Gently stack the roll-ups in the slow cooker.
- Pour the gravy over the top.
- Cover and cook on high for 1 to 1½ hours or on low for 2 to 3 hours.

Note: I cut these into two pieces, placing a toothpick in each end, and use them as a hot party snack. Everyone loves them. I get 32 bites.

Yield: 6 servings

Calories: 214; Fat: 2g (5% fat); Cholesterol: 34mg; Carbohydrate: 30g; Dietary Fiber: 0g; Protein: 20g; Sodium: 1484mg

★ **Turkey Roll-Ups:** Make as directed for Chicken Roll-Ups but substitute 1 (16-ounce) package of deli turkey slices and 1 (12-ounce) jar of roasted turkey gravy.

Calories: 196; Fat: 2g (5% fat); Cholesterol: 28mg; Carbohydrate: 28g; Dietary Fiber: 0g; Protein: 18g; Sodium: 1300mg

 Menu idea: Serve with Apple-Yam Casserole (page 86) and a tossed salad to complete this meal.

Cinnamon-Kissed Chicken

This chicken dish has a flavor of its own.

1/2 teaspoon ground cinnamon	1 teaspoon fresh orange zest*
1 tablespoon dark brown sugar	1 pound boneless, skinless
1/2 cup red wine vinegar, fat-free salad dressing	chicken breasts, cut into 1/2- by 4-inch-long strips

- Spray a slow cooker with nonfat cooking spray.
- In a bowl mix together the cinnamon, brown sugar, salad dressing, and orange zest.
- Place the chicken in the cooker and cover with the salad dressing mixture.
- Cover and cook on high for 3 to 4 hours or on low for 6 to 8 hours.

Yield: 4 (5-ounce) servings

*Note: To get orange peel zest, simply grate the peel of an orange with a vegetable peeler or paring knife. Use just the peel, not the white meaty part of the skin.

Calories: 154; Fat: 1g (9% fat); Cholesterol: 66mg; Carbohydrate: 7g; Dietary Fiber: 0g; Protein: 26g; Sodium: 475mg

 Menu idea: Simply add 4 small sweet potatoes into the slow cooker and then serve a fresh spinach salad garnished with Mandarin orange segments and your favorite fat-free salad dressing for a healthy meal that is as yummy as it is nutritious.

Dilled Chicken and Potatoes

The delicious dill flavor gently enhances, but does not overpower this entrée.

1	cup dill pickle juice	8 medium potatoes
2	pounds chicken breasts cut into 8 (4-ounce) steaks	Fresh dill, optional

- Spray a slow cooker with nonfat cooking spray.
- Place the pickle juice and chicken in the bottom of the cooker.
- Place the potatoes on top.
- Cover and cook on low for 7 to 8 hours or on high for 3 hours.
- If desired, sprinkle fresh dill on top before serving.

Yield: 8 servings (4 ounces meat and 1 potato)

Calories: 226; Fat: 1g (5% fat); Cholesterol: 66mg; Carbohydrate: 26g; Dietary Fiber: 3g; Protein: 30g; Sodium: 198mg

★ **Dilled Pork & Potatoes:** Substitute 2 pounds of pork tenderloin cut into 8 (4-ounce steaks) for the chicken. Cook on low for 7 to 8 hours or on high for 4½ hours.

Calories: 238; Fat: 4g (14% fat); Cholesterol: 74mg; Carbohydrate: 26g; Dietary Fiber: 3g; Protein: 28g; Sodium: 181mg

 Menu idea: The unique use of dill pickle juice in this recipe tastes especially good served with my Sassy Slaw and Peaches and Cream Gelatin Salad, both from *Busy People's Low-Fat Cookbook*.

Florentine Chicken Roll-Ups

If you like spinach, you'll like this creative dish.

4	skinless, boneless chicken breasts
2	tablespoons fat-free cream cheese, room temperature
1/4	cup reduced-fat Parmesan cheese
1	egg white
1	small onion, chopped
1	(10-ounce) package frozen chopped spinach, thawed and drained
1	cup fat-free sour cream
	Paprika, optional

- Spray a slow cooker with nonfat cooking spray.
- Put the chicken breasts between two pieces of waxed paper and flatten them with a rolling pin. (Use a full can of vegetables if you don't have a rolling pin.)
- In a bowl mix together the cream cheese, Parmesan, egg white, and chopped onion. Add the chopped spinach and mix well. Divide the mixture among the chicken breasts and roll up, securing with a toothpick.
- Place the rolled-up chicken in the cooker and pour the fat-free sour cream over the breasts.
- Cook on low for 4 hours.
- Sprinkle with paprika, if using, before serving.

Yield: 4 servings

Calories: 261; Fat: 3g (12% fat); Cholesterol: 71mg; Carbohydrate: 20g; Dietary Fiber: 2g; Protein: 35g; Sodium: 343mg

 Menu idea: Garlic Red Skins and Tomato Biscuits, both from *Busy People's Low-Fat Cookbook*, are a great flavor combination with this entrée along with a fresh garden salad.

Honey Mustard Chicken

This is a fantastic chicken recipe.

8	(4-ounce) boneless, skinless chicken breasts	2	cups fat-free honey-Dijon salad dressing

- Spray a slow cooker with nonfat cooking spray.
- Put the chicken in the slow cooker and cover it with the salad dressing.
- Cover and cook on high for 3 to 4 hours or on low for 6 to 8 hours.

Yield: 8 servings

Calories: 225; Fat: 1g (8% fat); Cholesterol: 66mg; Carbohydrate: 22g;
Dietary Fiber: 2g; Protein: 27g; Sodium: 734mg

 Menu idea: Making a double recipe of the Spiced Apples (page 112) and the Cottage Cheese Bread (page 35) and serving it along with the Spring Salad from *Busy People's Low-Fat Cookbook* makes an excellent meal.

Quick-Fix Chicken

Moist and juicy.

1 **pound boneless, skinless chicken breasts, cut into** ¹/₂-**inch-wide strips**	1 **cup fat-free coleslaw dressing (I use T. Marzetti's)** **Garlic salt, optional**

- Spray a slow cooker with nonfat cooking spray.
- In the slow cooker mix together the chicken breasts and coleslaw dressing.
- Cover and cook on low for 10 hours.
- Sprinkle lightly with garlic salt, if desired, and serve hot.

Yield: 5 (3-ounce) servings

Calories: 172; Fat: 1g (6% fat); Cholesterol: 77mg; Carbohydrate: 18g; Dietary Fiber: 0g; Protein: 21g; Sodium: 683mg

★ **Quick-Fix Steak:** Substitute for the chicken breasts 1 pound eye of round beef, cut into long, ¹/₂-inch-wide strips.

Calories: 192; Fat: 4g (19% fat); Cholesterol: 73mg; Carbohydrate: 18g; Dietary Fiber: 0g; Protein: 20g; Sodium: 672mg

★ **Quick-Fix Pork:** Substitute for the chicken 1 pound pork tenderloin cut into long, ¹/₂-inch-wide strips.

Calories: 181; Fat: 3g (16% fat); Cholesterol: 83mg; Carbohydrate: 18g; Dietary Fiber: 0g; Protein: 19g; Sodium: 669mg

★ **Quick-Fix Turkey:** Substitute for the chicken 1 pound boneless, skinless turkey breast cut into long, ¹/₂-inch-wide strips.

Calories: 172; Fat: 1g (5% fat); Cholesterol: 86mg; Carbohydrate: 18g; Dietary Fiber: 0g; Protein: 22g; Sodium: 664mg

 Menu idea: Serve with Baked Sweet Potatoes (page 89) and a fresh garden salad.

Tarragon Chicken & Potatoes

Sue Bucher, a friend, gave me this recipe idea. I really like it.

2	pounds boneless, skinless chicken breast	2	plus 2 tablespoons Butter Buds Sprinkles
1	teaspoon dried tarragon	5	large red-skin potatoes
1	teaspoon minced garlic		Light salt
			Ground pepper

- Spray a slow cooker with nonfat cooking spray.
- Rub the chicken with the dried tarragon, garlic, and 2 tablespoons of the Butter Buds Sprinkles. Place the chicken in the slow cooker.
- Place the potatoes on top of the chicken.
- Sprinkle the potatoes with the remaining 2 tablespoons Butter Buds Sprinkles.
- Cover and cook on low for 8 to 10 hours or on high for 4 to 5 hours.
- Lightly sprinkle the chicken with the light salt and ground pepper to taste before serving.

Yield: 5 (6-ounce) servings

Calories: 314; Fat: 2g (6% fat); Cholesterol: 105mg; Carbohydrate: 31g; Dietary Fiber: 3g; Protein: 46g; Sodium: 406mg

 Menu idea: Double the Mama's Beans recipe (page 110) and serve with Tomato Biscuits from *Busy People's Low-Fat Cookbook* for a meal that'll have them asking for seconds.

Turkey & Dressing Dinner

Turkey and dressing isn't just for the holidays anymore.

1 **(6-serving) box stuffing, chicken or turkey flavor**	1 **(12-ounce) jar fat-free turkey gravy**
1½ **cups hot water**	1 **(1-pound) bag frozen green beans**
1 **plus 1 (½-ounce) envelope Butter Buds Sprinkles, dry**	**Pepper, optional**
12 **ounces turkey breast lunchmeat**	

- Spray a slow cooker with nonfat cooking spray.
- In a medium bowl mix together the stuffing and seasoning, water, and 1 envelope of the Butter Buds.
- Spread the stuffing mixture evenly on the bottom of the slow cooker.
- Arrange the turkey lunchmeat slices on top of the stuffing. (The edges of the lunchmeat should overlap.)
- Spread the gravy evenly over the turkey.
- Evenly arrange the green beans on top of the gravy.
- Sprinkle the green beans with the remaining envelope of Butter Buds and pepper to taste.
- Cover and cook on low for 5 to 6 hours.

Yield: 5 servings

Calories: 257; Fat: 3g (10% fat); Cholesterol: 28mg; Carbohydrate: 42g; Dietary Fiber: 3g; Protein: 19g; Sodium: 1741mg

 Menu idea: This is good with Apple-Yam Casserole (page 86).

Beef & Mushroom Gravy Over Potatoes

The beef is super tender and cooked to perfection.

2 pounds eye of round, cut into $^1/_2$-inch pieces with all visible fat removed	1 (10$^3/_4$-ounce) can 98% fat-free cream of mushroom soup
1 cup fat-free, onion-flavored beef broth	1 (8-ounce) package sliced mushrooms, rinsed
1 (1-ounce) envelope dry onion soup mix	7 medium-size potatoes, washed

- Spray a slow cooker with nonfat cooking spray.
- In the cooker stir together the eye of round, beef broth, onion soup mix, mushroom soup, and mushrooms until well mixed.
- Put the potatoes on top.
- Cover and cook on high for 5 hours.
- Cut the potatoes in half lengthwise.
- Spoon 1 cup beef and mushroom gravy over the potatoes.

Yield: 7 servings (1 cup gravy and 1 potato)

Calories: 335; Fat: 7g (18% fat); Cholesterol: 72mg; Carbohydrate: 37g; Dietary Fiber: 4g; Protein: 35g; Sodium: 747mg

 Menu idea: I enjoy starting this meal off with a cup of hot Vegetable Hobo Soup (page 68) that I prepare in another slow cooker along with Pinwheel Dinner Rolls from *Busy People's Low-Fat Cookbook.*

Beef & Pasta Casserole

If you like beef and noodles, then you'll like this.

1¹/₂ cups uncooked elbow macaroni (Use only Mueller's brand.)	2 teaspoons minced garlic
1 (14-ounce) can fat-free beef broth	1 (12-ounce) can roast beef
	Salt
	Pepper

- Spray a slow cooker with nonfat cooking spray.
- Turn the cooker on high. In the cooker stir together the macaroni, beef broth, and garlic making sure all of the pasta is covered with the beef broth.
- Cover and cook on high for 1¹/₂ hours.
- Unplug the cooker.
- Stir in the roast beef.
- Cover and let sit for 5 minutes or until the beef is warm.
- If desired, add the salt and pepper to taste.

Note: I tried making this with different noodles but with no luck. Do not use the pasta from a macaroni and cheese box. It is too thin and will be mushy. Use elbow macaroni only.

Yield: 5 (1-cup) servings

Calories: 219; Fat: 5g (20% fat); Cholesterol: 46mg; Carbohydrate: 24g; Dietary Fiber: 1g; Protein: 19g; Sodium: 1000mg

 Menu idea: For a well balanced meal serve this with Broccoli Parmesan and Cucumber Dill Salad both from the *Busy People's Low-Fat Cookbook*.

Beef Burrito Casserole

A tasty twist to the traditional burrito.

2 (12-ounce) cans beef with gravy	½ pound fat-free cheddar cheese, cut into ½-inch squares
2 (15-ounce) cans fat-free chili	10 fat-free flour tortillas, torn into quarters

- Spray a slow cooker with nonfat cooking spray.
- In a medium-size bowl stir together the beef, chili, and cheese until well mixed.
- Starting with the mixture, alternate layers of one-third of the beef mixture and one-half of the tortillas in the slow cooker. Repeat the layers, ending with the beef mixture.
- Cover and cook on high for 2 to 4 hours or on low for 4 to 8 hours.

Yield: 12 (1-cup) servings

Calories: 279; Fat: 3g (10% fat); Cholesterol: 34mg; Carbohydrate: 31g; Dietary Fiber: 6g; Protein: 25g; Sodium: 705mg

 Menu idea: For a fun meal with a southwestern theme, serve with a taco salad.

Beef-N-Noodles

This is a great way to use leftover spaghetti noodles.

1	(12-ounce) jar fat-free seasoned pork or beef gravy	2	cups eye of round beef, cooked and shredded or 1 pound ground meatless burger (I use Morningstar Farms.)
2	cups pasta, cooked (Use only Mueller's brand.)		

- Spray a slow cooker with nonfat cooking spray.
- In the slow cooker mix together the gravy with the cooked pasta and beef.
- Cover and cook on low for 2½ hours.

*Note: Leftover spaghetti noodles will work if you have them. Just soak the cooked spaghetti completely covered in a bowl of water in the refrigerator until you need it for this recipe.

Yield: 4 (1-cup) servings

Calories: 240; Fat: 4g (15% fat); Cholesterol: 49mg; Carbohydrate: 24g; Dietary Fiber: 1g; Protein: 25g; Sodium: 525mg

 Menu idea: Green Bean and Onion Pocket Pouch (page 9) and fresh strawberries.

Beef Roast Excellenté

The ginger ale makes this tender and tasty. Don't worry; it's not sweet.

2	pounds eye of round roast, fat removed	6	medium potatoes
4	cups ginger ale (not diet)	3	large onions, cut into quarters
I	tablespoon minced garlic		Salt
			Pepper

- Spray a slow cooker with nonfat cooking spray.
- Place the roast in a slow cooker.
- Pour the ginger ale over the roast.
- Stir in the garlic.
- Place the potatoes and onions on top of the roast.
- Cover and cook on low for 7 to 9 hours or on high for 3½ to 4 hours.
- If desired, serve the juices on the side for dipping the meat.
- Salt and pepper to taste.

Yield: 6 servings (½ onion, 1 potato, and 4 ounces roast per serving)

Calories: 398; Fat: 7g (14% fat); Cholesterol: 82mg; Carbohydrate: 50g; Dietary Fiber: 5g; Protein: 38g; Sodium: 95mg

★ **Pork Roast Excellenté:** Substitute 2 pounds pork tenderloin for the beef.

Calories: 379; Fat: 5g (12% fat); Cholesterol: 98mg; Carbohydrate: 50g; Dietary Fiber: 5g; Protein: 37g; Sodium: 91mg

 Menu idea: This is good served with a tossed salad and dinner rolls.

Beef Stroganoff Casserole

If you like beef stroganoff, you'll like this.

1½ cups uncooked elbow macaroni (Use only Mueller's brand.)	1 (6½-ounce) can mushroom stems and pieces, drained
1 (14-ounce) can fat-free beef broth	½ cup fat-free sour cream
1 (12-ounce) can roast beef	Salt
2 teaspoons minced garlic	Pepper

- Spray a slow cooker with nonfat cooking spray.
- Turn the cooker on high. Put the macaroni and beef broth in the cooker, making sure all the pasta is covered with the beef broth.
- Cover and cook on high for 1½ hours.
- Stir in the roast beef, minced garlic, mushrooms, and sour cream.
- Cover and let sit for 5 minutes or until everything is completely heated.
- Salt and pepper to taste, if desired.

Note: Noodles don't work. Use elbow macaroni only and not the macaroni from a macaroni and cheese mix.

Yield: 7 (1-cup) servings

Calories: 183; Fat: 4g (18% fat); Cholesterol: 33mg; Carbohydrate: 22g; Dietary Fiber: 1g; Protein: 15g; Sodium: 825mg

 Menu idea: Serve this with a fresh tossed salad to complement the meal.

Chili Mac

Surprise! This easy-to-put-together entrée is vegetarian, but if you don't tell people, they'll never know.

4 cups hot water	1 pound elbow macaroni (Use only Mueller's brand.)
1 (12-ounce) package cooked ground beef substitute found in frozen food section* (I use Morningstar Farms.)	1 (15-ounce) can fat-free, spicy vegetarian chili with black beans (I use Health Valley.)

- Spray a slow cooker with nonfat cooking spray.
- In the slow cooker stir together the water and ground beef substitute.
- Cover and cook for 1 hour on high.
- Add the macaroni and cook ½ hour more.
- Stir in the chili just before serving.

Note: Cooked ground beef substitute tastes like cooked ground hamburger, but it is 78 percent lower in fat.

Note: If desired, you can substitute 12 ounces of ground eye of round. Simply brown the meat in a skillet before adding it to the slow cooker.

Yield: 10 (1-cup) servings

Calories: 238; Fat: 1g (3% fat); Cholesterol: 0mg; Carbohydrate: 42g; Dietary Fiber: 5g; Protein: 15g; Sodium: 179mg

Menu idea: This flavorful casserole tastes fabulous with southwestern style side dishes such as Taco Vegetable Soup (page 62) and Southwestern Three Beans (page 75).

Cowboy Chow

Cowboys of the olden days only wish it would have tasted this good. For fun, serve in pie pans instead of plates with gingham napkins.

14	ounces low-fat smoked sausage, cut into bite-size pieces	1	(15 ½-ounce) can dark red kidney beans, drained
1	cup chunky salsa	1	(53-ounce) can pork and beans, drained and remove all visible chunks of fat
1	cup barbecue sauce		
1	(10-ounce) can whole kernel corn, drained	½	cup chopped onion (for faster preparation use frozen chopped onions)

- Spray a slow cooker with nonfat cooking spray.
- In the cooker stir together the sausage, salsa, barbecue sauce, corn, kidney beans, pork and beans, and onion until well mixed.
- Cover and cook on low 3 to 6 hours.

Yield: 9 (1-cup) servings

Calories: 294; Fat: 4g (11% fat); Cholesterol: 26mg; Carbohydrate: 51g; Dietary Fiber: 11g; Protein: 17g; Sodium: 1528mg

 Menu idea: Serve with fresh sliced tomatoes and cucumbers, whole wheat bread, and watermelon slices.

Cowboy Grub (Casserole)

For a cowboy theme, serve this in tin pie plates with bandanas as napkins.

1 pound eye of round beef, cut into ¼-inch cubes	½ cup frozen chopped onion
1 pound fat-free shredded hash browns	¾ cup barbecue sauce

- Spray a slow cooker with nonfat cooking spray.
- In the cooker stir together the beef, hash browns, onion, and barbecue sauce until well mixed.
- Cover and cook on low for 9 to 10 hours or on high for 4½ hours.

Yield: 4 (1-cup) servings

Calories: 284; Fat: 6g (18% fat); Cholesterol: 61mg; Carbohydrate: 30g; Dietary Fiber: 4g; Protein: 28g; Sodium: 478mg

 Menu idea: This is good served with coleslaw and green beans.

Cube Steak with Mushroom Gravy & Potatoes

This is one of my favorite ways to prepare cube steak.

2 (12-ounce) jars mushroom gravy	1/4 teaspoon ground black pepper
2 (7-ounce) cans mushroom stems and pieces, drained	6 (4-ounce) cube steaks
1/2 teaspoon thyme	6 medium potatoes, washed and cut into 1/2-inch cubes

- Spray a slow cooker with nonfat cooking spray.
- Put the gravy, mushrooms, thyme, and pepper in the cooker and stir until well mixed.
- Mix the meat into the gravy and then mix the potatoes, with the skin facing up, into the gravy.
- Cover and cook on high for 3 to 4 hours or on low for 7½ to 8½ hours.
- Remove the meat and place on serving plates.
- With a slotted spoon remove the potatoes and mushrooms and place them together in a serving bowl. Serve the gravy on the side.

Yield: 6 servings (4 ounces beef, 1 medium potato, and mushroom gravy per serving)

Calories: 297; Fat: 5g (14% fat); Cholesterol: 61mg; Carbohydrate: 34g; Dietary Fiber: 4g; Protein: 32g; Sodium: 908mg

 Menu idea: Serve this with a Green Bean and Onion Pocket Pouch (page 9) and sourdough rolls.

Herbed Beef Tenderloin with Seasoned Potatoes & Buttered Mushrooms

Put into a slow cooker before a long day away and come home to a mouth-watering aroma that's delicious and ready to eat.

2 pounds beef tenderloin, fat removed	**1 pound bag frozen, seasoned diced potatoes**
1¹/₂ teaspoons dried thyme	**2 plus 1 tablespoons fat-free margarine**
1¹/₂ teaspoons dried basil	
1 teaspoon garlic salt	**6 ounces fresh sliced mushrooms**

- Spray a slow cooker with nonfat cooking spray.
- Rub all sides of the beef with the basil, thyme, and garlic salt.
- Place the beef tenderloin on the outer rim edge of the slow cooker. The center will be hollow.
- Take 2 pieces of foil about 18 inches long.
- Fold the seams together along the side.
- Spray the foil with nonfat cooking spray.
- Place the diced potatoes in the center of the foil. Spread 2 tablespoons of the margarine over the frozen diced potatoes.
- Fold the foil (as you would a gift package) to seal in the flavor of the potatoes.
- Place the potatoes in the center of the slow cooker and beef.
- Spray another 18 inches of foil with nonfat cooking spray.
- Place the mushrooms in the foil. Dab 1 tablespoon of fat-free margarine on top of the mushrooms.
- Sprinkle lightly with the garlic salt if desired.
- Fold the foil (as you would a gift package) to seal in flavor.
- Place the mushrooms on top of the potatoes and beef.
- Cover the cooker and cook on low for 8 to 10 hours or on high for 4 to 5 hours.
- Serve the juices in bottom of slow cooker on the side.

Yield: 6 servings (5 ounces beef, 1 ounce mushrooms, and ¹/₃ cup potatoes per serving)

Calories: 317; Fat: 11g (32% fat); Cholesterol: 94mg; Carbohydrate: 19g; Dietary Fiber: 2g; Protein: 34g; Sodium: 434mg

 Menu idea: This is good served with tossed salad and dinner rolls.

Meatloaf Dinner

What's better than a meat and potato dinner all in one pot?

2 egg whites	1/4 cup ketchup
1/4 cup skim milk	8 medium carrots, peeled and cut
2 slices day-old bread, cubed	into 1-inch cubes
1/3 cup chunky salsa	12 small red potatoes
1 1/2 pounds ground eye of round beef	

- Spray a slow cooker with nonfat cooking spray.
- In a bowl beat together the egg whites and milk.
- Stir in the bread cubes and salsa.
- Add the beef and mix well.
- Shape the beef mixture into a round loaf and place it in a slow cooker.
- Spread the ketchup on top of the loaf.
- Place the carrots and potatoes on top.
- Cover and cook on high for 1 hour.
- Reduce the heat to low and cook for 7 to 8 hours longer until the meat is no longer pink in the center and the vegetables are tender.

Yield: 6 servings (4 ounces meatloaf, 1¼ carrots, and 2 potatoes)

Calories: 324; Fat: 11g (30% fat); Cholesterol: 42mg; Carbohydrate: 28g; Dietary Fiber: 5g; Protein: 28g; Sodium: 380mg

 Menu idea: Since these vegetables are high in carbohydrates, I suggest having a fresh garden salad with this meal.

Mexican Goulash

When I created this, the flavor and texture turned out better than I thought it would.

I	(15-ounce) can fat-free chili (made with turkey)	1½ cups salsa	
I	(16-ounce) can fat-free refried beans	I	cup fat-free fancy shredded cheddar cheese, optional
I	(12-ounce) can whole kernel corn, drained	5	(10-inch) fat-free flour tortillas

- Spray a slow cooker with nonfat cooking spray.
- In a large bowl stir together the chili, refried beans, corn, and salsa until well mixed.
- Lay one tortilla flat on the bottom of the slow cooker.
- Pour one-fifth of the mixture on top.
- Continue layering the tortillas and the remaining four-fifths of the mixture until all the ingredients are used.
- Cover and cook on low for 7 hours.
- Using a sharp knife (a steak knife works well) cut through all the layers, making a checkerboard design on top. Each cut should be about 1-inch apart. (The cut-up tortillas will taste a lot like pasta when the recipe is finished.)
- With a large spoon stir the entire dish to mix the cut-up tortilla pieces.
- Serve in soup bowls.
- Sprinkle lightly with additional fat-free cheddar cheese, if desired.

Yield: 8 (1-cup) servings

Calories: 232; Fat: 2g (7% fat); Cholesterol: 7mg; Carbohydrate: 42g; Dietary Fiber: 7g; Protein: 11g; Sodium: 968mg

 Menu idea: A tossed salad rounds out this meal, and sugar-free vanilla pudding ends it nicely.

Roast Beef Dumpling Casserole

I was so happy when I figured out how to cook noodles in the slow cooker. You'll be pleased, too.

3	cups hot water	3	(12-ounce) jars fat-free beef gravy
8	ounces fat-free shredded cheddar cheese	I	(16-ounce) can mixed vegetables, drained
I	(4-ounce) jar mushrooms, drained	I	(12-ounce) bag eggless dumplings (Use only No-Yolk.)
2	(12-ounce) cans roast beef		

- Spray a slow cooker with nonfat cooking spray.
- In the slow cooker mix together the water, cheese, mushrooms, roast beef, gravy, and vegetables.
- Add the Spiced Apples Pocket Pouch at this time if you are making them with this entrée.
- Cover and cook on low for 8 hours.
- If making the Spiced Apples, remove them from the slow cooker.
- Turn to high, cover, and cook for 5 minutes.
- Stir in the dumplings, making sure dumplings are completely covered with liquid.
- Continue cooking for ½ hour more or until the dumplings are tender.

Note: If some of the dumplings accidentally rise above the liquid and become dry, simply remove those few dumplings with a slotted spoon before serving.

Yield: 12 (1-cup) servings

Calories: 220; Fat: 2g (9% fat); Cholesterol: 21mg; Carbohydrate: 32g; Dietary Fiber: 3g; Protein: 17g; Sodium: 1065mg

 Menu idea: The Spiced Apples (page 112) complements this casserole, but a 6-quart or larger slow cooker is needed if you are making the Spiced Apples as a pocket pouch.

Roast Beef Open-Faced Sandwiches with Gravy and Mashed Potatoes

This is an old country favorite.

2 (15-ounce) cans whole potatoes, not drained	1/2 cup skim milk
1 pound extra lean sliced roast beef	2 ounces fat-free cream cheese
2 (12-ounce) jars fat-free beef-flavored gravy	1 tablespoon reduced-fat margarine
	5 slices fat-free white bread

- Put both cans of potatoes in the bottom of a slow cooker.
- Make a bowl out of heavy-duty (18-inch-wide) aluminum foil by pressing the foil into the slow cooker. Let the bottom of the foil bowl rest on top of the potatoes. Fold the remaining foil over the edge of the cooker and let the extra foil overhang on the outside of the slow cooker.
- Gently stir together the meat and gravy into the foil bowl.
- Cover and cook on low for 3 hours.
- Remove the foil bowl of meat and gravy.
- Drain the water from the potatoes.
- In the slow cooker add to the potatoes the milk, cream cheese, and margarine. Break up the potatoes. With the mixer on medium speed beat together all of the ingredients in the slow cooker to make mashed potatoes. If desired more milk can be added.
- Set out five dinner plates. On each plate place 1 slice of bread. Put 1 cup of the meat and gravy on the bread and 1/2 cup of the mashed potatoes next to it. Serve immediately.

Yield: 5 servings (1 cup gravy, 1/2 cup mashed potatoes, and 1 slice bread per serving)

Calories: 309; Fat: 4g (12% fat); Cholesterol: 41mg; Carbohydrate: 44g; Dietary Fiber: 3g; Protein: 25g; Sodium: 2121mg

 Menu idea: It doesn't get any easier than this folks! For a well-balanced meal simply serve with one of your favorite green vegetables such as steamed green beans or cooked spinach.

Smothered Steak

Each succulent bite is as tasty as the one before.

1	pound beef tenderloin, whole	8	ounces fresh mushrooms, sliced
2	large onions, quartered and separated	1/4	cup Butter Buds, dry
2	large green peppers, cut into 3/4-inch strips	1/2	cup water
		1	teaspoon celery salt or garlic salt

- Spray a slow cooker with nonfat cooking spray.
- Place the beef in the bottom of the cooker and top with the onions, green peppers, and mushrooms.
- In a bowl mix the Butter Buds, water, and garlic salt together until the Butter Buds are dissolved. Pour over the vegetables.
- Gently toss the vegetables to distribute the seasonings.
- Cover and cook on high for 4 to 5 hours or on low for 8 to 9 hours.
- Cut the beef into 4 steaks.
- Arrange the steaks on a platter.
- Toss the vegetables in the juices before pouring the juice and vegetables over the beef.
- Serve hot.

Yield: 4 servings (4 ounces steak, 1/2 onion, 1/2 green pepper, and 2 ounces mushrooms per serving)

Calories: 270; Fat: 9g (28% fat); Cholesterol: 70mg; Carbohydrate: 23g; Dietary Fiber: 4g; Protein: 27g; Sodium: 656mg

★ **Smothered Chicken:** Substitute 4 (4-ounce) boneless, skinless chicken breasts with all fat removed for the beef tenderloin.

Calories: 217; Fat: 2g (7% fat); Cholesterol: 66mg; Carbohydrate: 23g; Dietary Fiber: 4g; Protein: 30g; Sodium: 677mg

 Menu idea: When served with Mashed Potatoes Deluxe and Pinwheel Dinner Rolls, from *Busy People's Low-Fat Cookbook*, this is a meal combination that'll have everyone happy when they come to your table to eat.

Spiced Steak & Beans

When you are trying to think of something different and delicious to fix, this recipe will pop into your mind. Expect compliments.

1½ pounds eye-of-round beef steak
1 tablespoon prepared mustard
1 tablespoon chili powder
2 (14½-ounce) cans diced low-sodium tomatoes
1 medium onion, chopped
1 beef bouillon cube, crushed
1 (16-ounce) can kidney beans, rinsed and drained
1 (14½-ounce) can cut green beans, drained

- Spray a slow cooker with nonfat cooking spray.
- Cut the steak into thin strips.
- In a bowl stir together the mustard and chili powder until well mixed.
- Add the steak and coat well with the mixture.
- Put the steak into the cooker.
- Add the tomatoes, onion, and bouillon.
- Cover and cook on low for 6 to 8 hours.
- Stir in the beans.
- Cover and cook for another 30 minutes or until the beans are hot.

Yield: 8 (1-cup) servings

Calories: 200; Fat: 4g (19% fat); Cholesterol: 46mg; Carbohydrate: 17g; Dietary Fiber; 6g; Protein: 23g; Sodium: 420mg

 Menu idea: Serve this over cooked rice for a complete meal.

Stuffed Green Peppers

Talk about quick to prepare. It doesn't get any easier than this.

4 large fresh green peppers	2 cups vegetable juice, mild picante flavor or regular flavor
1 pound ground eye of round (or ground turkey breast)	
2 cups instant long-grain white rice	2 (14 1/2-ounce) cans sliced, stewed tomatoes

- Spray a slow cooker with nonfat cooking spray.
- Cut the tops off the green peppers and discard.
- Clean out the insides of the green peppers and set the peppers aside.
- In a bowl mix the ground eye of round, rice, and vegetable juice together.
- Stuff the peppers with the beef/rice mixture.
- Arrange the stuffed peppers in the slow cooker. Arrange the sliced, stewed tomatoes on top of and around the peppers in bottom of the slow cooker.
- Cover and cook on high for 4 hours or on low for 8 to 9 hours.
- When serving, cut each pepper in half horizontally. Lay each pepper on a plate on its side with the beef/rice mixture facing up. Spoon stewed tomatoes and the juices in the bottom of the slow cooker on top of each pepper.

Yield: 4 servings (1 pepper each)

Calories: 499; Fat: 11g (20% fat); Cholesterol: 41mg; Carbohydrate: 69g; Dietary Fiber: 6g; Protein: 31g; Sodium: 852mg

 Menu idea: This is a complete meal in itself. However, if desired, serve with a fresh garden salad.

Swiss Steak & Potatoes

What a wonderful, warm, and mouth-watering meal to come home to on a cold or chilly day.

1	(14½-ounce) can stewed, sliced tomatoes, not drained	1	(1-pound) bag fresh mini carrots
1	(12-ounce) jar fat-free, beef-flavored gravy	2	medium onions, quartered
		1	pound eye of round beef steaks, cut to ½-inch thickness
¼	teaspoon dried thyme	4	medium potatoes, washed

- Spray a slow cooker with nonfat cooking spray.
- In the cooker stir the stewed tomatoes, gravy, thyme, carrots, and onions together until well mixed.
- Place the meat into the mixture, making sure it is completely covered with the sauce.
- Place the potatoes on top.
- Cover and cook on high for 4 hours or on low for 8 hours. It's completely cooked after the documented time; however, the meal can remain in the slow cooker for up to 1 hour longer without burning.

Yield: 4 servings (4 ounces beef, 4 ounces carrots, ½ onion, 1 potato, and ¾ cup gravy per serving)

Calories: 374; Fat: 6g (13% fat); Cholesterol: 61mg; Carbohydrate: 54g; Dietary Fiber: 8g; Protein: 33g; Sodium: 783mg

 Menu idea: I really like eating this with Tomato Biscuits and Spring Asparagus, both from *Busy People's Low-Fat Cookbook.*

Teriyaki Beef

This is so moist, tender, and delicious, my mouth waters just thinking of it.

¹/₃ cup Kikkoman's Teriyaki Baste & Glaze	**1¹/₂ pounds boneless beef chuck steak**
1 (10-ounce) can crushed pineapple, not drained	

- Spray a slow cooker with nonfat cooking spray.
- In the cooker mix together the Baste & Glaze and the pineapple.
- Remove all the visible fat from the beef. Saturate the meat in the teriyaki mixture.
- Cook on low for 2¹/₂ to 3¹/₂ hours.

Yield: 6 (¹/₂-cup) servings

Calories: 214; Fat: 6g (26% fat); Cholesterol: 79mg; Carbohydrate: 11g; Dietary Fiber: 0g; Protein: 26g; Sodium: 416mg

 Menu idea: Serve this with an Oriental Blend Pocket Pouch (page 9) and Pinwheel Dinner Rolls from *Busy People's Low-Fat Cookbook.*

Barbecue Pork Sandwiches

This barbecue melts in your mouth. I like to start this recipe before I go to bed, so when I wake up it's all ready once I shred the meat. I keep it in the slow cooker on warm until lunch.

2 **pounds pork tenderloin or pork tenderloin tips, all fat removed**	¹/₂ **cup frozen chopped onion**
1 **(16-ounce) bottle barbecue sauce**	13 **hamburger buns**

- Spray a slow cooker with nonfat cooking spray.
- Place into the cooker the pork tenderloin, barbecue sauce, and onion. Make sure the meat is completely covered in the sauce.
- Cover and cook on low for 7 to 9 hours. Remove the meat.
- With two forks pull across the grain of the meat to shred it.
- Return the torn meat to the slow cooker.
- Stir the meat until it is saturated with barbecue sauce.
- Place ¹/₃ cup barbecue on each bun.

Yield: 13 (¹/₃-cup) servings

Calories: 234; Fat: 5g (21% fat); Cholesterol: 45mg; Carbohydrate: 26g; Dietary Fiber: 2g; Protein: 19g; Sodium: 561mg

★ **Barbecue Chicken Sandwiches:** Substitute 2 pounds boneless, skinless chicken breasts with all fat removed for the pork tenderloin.

Calories: 227; Fat: 4g (15% fat); Cholesterol: 40mg; Carbohydrate: 26g; Dietary Fiber: 2g; Protein: 20g; Sodium: 571mg

★ **Barbecue Beef Sandwiches:** Substitute 2 pounds eye of round beef with all fat removed for the pork tenderloin.

Calories: 242; Fat: 6g (22% fat); Cholesterol: 38mg; Carbohydrate: 26g; Dietary Fiber: 2g; Protein: 19g; Sodium: 563mg

 Menu idea: This is good with Sassy Slaw and Cucumber Dill Salad, from *Busy People's Low-Fat Cookbook*. Along with your favorite pickles, it adds more fun to these zesty sandwiches.

Cabbage Rolls

Put the cabbage in the freezer until frozen. (I do this days, even weeks, ahead of time.) The leaves will become soft, once thawed. No need to precook the leaves.

1 **(14-ounce) fat-free kielbasa, cut into ¼-inch pieces**	2 **(10½-ounce) cans condensed tomato soup—Do not make as directed on can. Reserve 2 tablespoons**
1 **cup cooked instant rice**	
¼ **cup chopped onion, frozen or fresh**	8 **large cabbage leaves with stems cut off**
2 **egg whites**	

- Spray a slow cooker with nonfat cooking spray.
- In the cooker mix together the kielbasa, cooked rice, onion, egg whites, and the 2 tablespoons condensed soup until well mixed.
- Place ⅓ cup of the mixture on each cabbage leaf.
- Roll up the leaves and secure each one with a toothpick.
- Place the leaves in the slow cooker.
- Cover the leaves with the remaining condensed soup.
- Cover and cook on high for 2½ to 3 hours or on low for 5 or 6 hours or until the cabbage is tender.

Yield: 4 servings (2 cabbage rolls per serving)

Calories: 315; Fat: 0g (0% fat); Cholesterol: 43mg; Carbohydrate: 56g; Dietary Fiber: 4g; Protein: 22g; Sodium: 2098mg

 Menu idea: Serve this with a tossed salad and sliced pears.

California Medley Stew

This hearty stew is very filling.

4	medium-size potatoes, not peeled, cut in 1/2-inch chunks
1	medium onion, chopped in 1 1/2-inch slices or 1 cup frozen chopped onion
2	(14-ounce) packages low-fat smoked sausage, cut into 1/2-inch cubes
2	(1/2-ounce) envelopes Butter Buds or 2 tablespoons Butter Buds Sprinkles
2	(14-ounce) cans fat-free chicken broth
1	pound California blend frozen vegetables
1/2	cup cornstarch
1	teaspoon garlic salt, optional

- Spray a slow cooker with nonfat cooking spray.
- In the cooker put the potatoes and onions first and top with the sausage, Butter Buds, and chicken broth. (It is completely fine if these ingredients are frozen when put into the slow cooker.)
- Cover and cook on low for 9 to 10 hours.
- Add the frozen vegetables and cook another hour.
- Drain the broth from the cooker and put all but 1 cup into a large, nonstick soup pan over high heat.
- Whisk the cornstarch with 1 cup of the broth and garlic salt.
- Once completely dissolved, stir the cornstarch mixture into the broth in a nonstick soup pan. With the whisk, keep stirring until the gravy is thick, about 4 to 5 minutes.
- Gently stir in the meat and vegetables from the slow cooker into the thick gravy.
- Serve immediately.

Note: Leftovers can be frozen and reheated in a microwave for a fast and easy meal.

Yield: 8 (1 1/4-cup) servings

Calories: 243; Fat: 3g (10% fat); Cholesterol: 35mg; Carbohydrate: 40g; Dietary Fiber: 3g; Protein: 17g; Sodium: 1273mg

 Menu idea: Serve this with a tossed salad and canned apricots.

Farmer's Casserole

This sensational casserole is a sure-fire winner with everyone, including farming families and city slickers.

1½ pounds extra lean ham, cut into bite-size cubes	1 (10¾-ounce) can 98% fat-free cream of mushroom soup
1 (20-ounce) package seasoned, diced potato home fries	½ cup chopped red onion or chopped frozen regular onions
1 (4-ounce) can mushroom stems and pieces, drained	1 (14½-ounce) can green beans, drained

- Spray a slow cooker with nonfat cooking spray.
- Place the ham, home fries, mushrooms, soup, onion, and green beans into the cooker and mix until well blended.
- Cover and cook on low for 4 hours.

Yield: 7 servings

Calories: 278; Fat: 9g (28% fat); Cholesterol: 50mg; Carbohydrate: 26g; Dietary Fiber: 3g; Protein: 23g; Sodium: 1732mg

 Menu idea: The Bacon, Lettuce, and Tomato Tossed Salad from *Busy People's Low-Fat Cookbook* easily completes this meal in a tasty way.

Ham & Cabbage Dinner

As a child this was one of my favorite meals. It's great to prepare when camping—if you're fortunate enough to have electricity when you camp. Some people like to put fresh peeled carrots and chunks of onions in this dish.

1 **(14-ounce) can fat-free chicken broth**	1 **head cabbage with core removed, cut into 6 wedges**
2 **tablespoons Butter Buds Sprinkles or 1 (¹/2-ounce) envelope Butter Buds**	¹/4 **cup fat-free butter spread** **Light salt** **Pepper**
1¹/2 **pounds extra lean ham**	

- In a slow cooker stir the Butter Buds with the chicken broth until dissolved.
- Put the cabbage wedges in the bottom of the slow cooker. Don't worry if the broth does not cover the cabbage.
- Place the chunk of ham on top of the cabbage.
- Cover and cook on low for 8 to 10 hours. Don't worry about overcooking.
- Cut the ham into 6 slices.
- Stir the cooked cabbage wedges in the broth before removing from the slow cooker.
- With a slotted spoon remove the cabbage and place it in a serving bowl.
- Toss with the butter spread. If desired, sprinkle lightly with the salt and pepper to taste.
- Serve immediately with the ham.

Yield: 6 servings

Calories: 206; Fat: 6g (26% fat); Cholesterol: 53mg; Carbohydrate: 14g; Dietary Fiber: 3g; Protein: 25g; Sodium: 1960 mg

 Menu idea: Microwaved red-skin potatoes taste good with sliced, fat-free wheat bread. (Aunt Millie's brand is good.) A mousse of any flavor, which is easy to prepare and complements this meal, is a rich and satisfying dessert. If you have an extra large slow cooker, go ahead and put the potatoes in before cooking, along with everything else.

Ham & Yam Casserole

A great way to use holiday leftovers. This has a really good flavor.

1 (40-ounce) can yams in syrup, drained	1 (20-ounce) can pineapple chunks in juice, drained
1½ pounds extra lean smoked ham, cut into bite-size cubes	¼ cup dark brown sugar

- Spray a slow cooker with nonfat cooking spray.
- In the cooker very gently stir together the drained yams, ham, drained pineapple, and brown sugar.
- Cover and cook on high for 1½ to 2 hours or on low for 4 to 6 hours.

Yield: 5 (1⅓-cup) servings

Calories: 467; Fat: 7g (14% fat); Cholesterol: 64mg; Carbohydrate: 71g; Dietary Fiber: 6g; Protein: 29g; Sodium: 2055mg

 Menu idea: This is good served with a fresh garden salad.

Ham Casserole

You won't believe how flavorful and easy this casserole is.

1½ pounds extra lean ham, cut into bite-size chunks

1 (20-ounce) package seasoned diced potatoes

1 (4-ounce) can mushroom stems and pieces, juices drained

1 (10³/4-ounce) can 98% fat-free cream of mushroom soup

5 ounces water (½ can)

½ cup chopped red onion (or chopped frozen regular onions)

1 (14½-ounce) can green beans, drained

- Spray a slow cooker with nonfat cooking spray.
- In the cooker stir the ham, potatoes, mushrooms, soup, water, onion, and green beans and mix until well blended.
- Cover and cook on low for 4 hours.

Yield: 7 (1¼-cup) servings

Calories: 232; Fat: 5g (20% fat); Cholesterol: 46mg; Carbohydrate: 24g; Dietary Fiber: 3g; Protein: 23g; Sodium: 1699mg

 Menu idea: This recipe is complete with carbohydrates and lean protein. If you have a sweet tooth, you can finish with a dessert of fresh fruit salad made of assorted melons.

Lemon Pepper Pork Tenderloin with Lemon-Kissed Potatoes

Put in right before leaving for church. There's nothing like coming home to a delicious home-cooked meal that's awaiting you.

2	pounds pork tenderloin with all visible fat removed	8	medium potatoes diced into $^1/_2$-inch cubes
2	medium lemons cut into quarters, discarding seeds	I	cup water
I	teaspoon ground pepper	I	teaspoon cream of tartar
I	teaspoon garlic salt	I	teaspoon dried parsley

- Spray a slow cooker with nonfat cooking spray.
- With a knife cut the pork tenderloin down the center lengthwise to divide it in half. Cut $^1/_4$-inch deep cuts all over the pork.
- Squeeze the lemon juice onto the tenderloin and sprinkle it lightly with the pepper and garlic salt.
- Put the meat in the slow cooker.
- Put the diced potatoes in a bowl with the water and cream of tartar. Let them soak for 1 minute. This will keep the potatoes from turning brown or getting discolored while cooking.
- Put the potatoes on top of meat in the slow cooker.
- Sprinkle with the parsley.
- Arrange any remaining lemon quarters on top.
- Cook on high for $2^1/_2$ to 3 hours or on low for 6 to 8 hours.
- Remove the lemons before serving.
- Serve on a large serving plate. If desired, you can sprinkle the potatoes lightly with salt and more dried parsley.

Yield: 8 servings (4 ounces pork and 1 potato)

Calories: 243; Fat: 4g (14% fat); Cholesterol: 67mg; Carbohydrate: 27g; Dietary Fiber: 3g; Protein: 28g; Sodium: 275mg

 Menu idea: Serve this with a California Blend Pocket Pouch (page 8).

Pigs Out of the Blanket

If you like pigs in the blanket you'll like this. It's just as delicious and a lot less time consuming to prepare.

1	pound ground eye of round beef	2	cups vegetable juice
2	cups instant long-grain white rice	1	(16-ounce) bag coleslaw mix (found in the produce section, it has cabbage and carrots)
1	(16-ounce) jar salsa (remember, the spicier your salsa the spicier your dish)	2	(14¹/₂-ounce) cans stewed tomatoes

- Spray a slow cooker with nonfat cooking spray.
- In the slow cooker, mix together* the beef, rice, salsa, vegetable juice, and coleslaw. (Remove any large pieces of cabbage and discard.)
- Cover and cook on high for 4 hours.
- When ready to serve, heat the stewed tomatoes in the microwave until they are heated through.
- Evenly pour the tomatoes over each serving.

Note: I find it's easiest to mix with my hands.

Yield: 6 (1-cup) servings

Calories: 350; Fat: 7g (19% fat); Cholesterol: 28mg; Carbohydrate: 46g; Dietary Fiber: 4g; Protein: 20g; Sodium: 941mg

 Menu idea: This is a meal in itself. It's also good served with sugar-free Jell-O or a piece of fruit if desired.

Pork Roast—Old-Fashioned Style

An old-time favorite made a lot *easier.*

2	(16-ounce) bags frozen vegetables for stew	1 1/2	pounds pork tenderloin
1	(14 1/2-ounce) can stewed tomatoes	1/3	cup flour
1	(10 3/4-ounce) can 98% fat-free cream of celery soup	1/4	cup water
			Garlic salt
1	teaspoon dried thyme or 2 teaspoons fresh thyme		Pepper

- Spray a slow cooker with nonfat cooking spray.
- In the slow cooker mix together the vegetables, stewed tomatoes, soup, and thyme until well blended.
- Push the pork down to the bottom and sides of the cooker.
- Cover and cook on low for 8 to 10 hours or on high 4 to 5 hours.
- Remove the vegetables and separate the potatoes, carrots, and pork. Leave the juice in the cooker and turn it on high.
- In a small bowl mix the flour and water together to make a thick paste.
- Stir the paste into the juices in the slow cooker until well blended.
- Cover and cook on high for 5 minutes or until thick.
- Add garlic salt and pepper to taste.

Yield: 6 servings (4 ounces pork, 1/2 cup vegetables, and 1/2 cup gravy)

Calories: 297; Fat: 5g (15% fat); Cholesterol: 76mg; Carbohydrate: 34g ; Dietary Fiber: 2g; Protein: 28g; Sodium: 488mg

 Menu idea: A complete meal. If desired, serve rye rolls on the side along with a tossed salad and peach-flavored applesauce.

Pork Enchilada Casserole

Slightly spicy and oh, so good.

2 (10-ounce) cans mild enchilada sauce	1 (8-ounce) bag fat-free shredded cheddar cheese
1½ pounds precooked, lean, shredded pork tenderloin	1 (11-ounce) package fat-free tortillas
1 cup fat-free sour cream	

- Spray a slow cooker with nonfat cooking spray.
- In a large bowl mix the enchilada sauce, pork, and sour cream together until the shredded pork and the sauce is well blended.
- Place one-fourth of each of the following in layers in the slow cooker: sauce, cheese, and tortillas. Some of the tortillas have to be torn in order to fill in the gaps between the whole tortillas and the edge of the slow cooker. End with the sauce on top.
- Cover and cook on low for 2 to 2½ hours. This recipe does not do well cooked on high.
- Cut the casserole into six pieces.

Yield: 6 servings

Calories: 459; Fat: 8g (17% fat); Cholesterol: 94mg; Carbohydrate: 41g; Dietary Fiber: 2g; Protein: 50g; Sodium: 1047mg

 Menu idea: For a fun meal with a southwestern theme start with Taco Soup from *Busy People's Low-Fat Cookbook* and a side salad of shredded lettuce, chopped tomatoes, salsa, crushed tortilla chips, and your favorite fat-free ranch dressing.

Pork Tenderloin

This is excellent for the holidays instead of the traditional ham or turkey.

1/4 cup whole-berry cranberry sauce	2 pounds pork tenderloin
1/4 cup apricot preserves	

- Spray a slow cooker with nonfat cooking spray.
- In the cooker mix together the cranberry sauce and apricot preserves until well blended.
- Spread the glaze over the pork tenderloin and place the tenderloin in the slow cooker.
- Cover and cook on low for 7½ to 9½ hours.

Yield: 8 (4-ounce) servings

Calories: 173; Fat: 4g (21% fat); Cholesterol: 74mg; Carbohydrate: 10g; Dietary Fiber: 0g; Protein: 24g; Sodium: 63mg

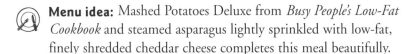 **Menu idea:** Mashed Potatoes Deluxe from *Busy People's Low-Fat Cookbook* and steamed asparagus lightly sprinkled with low-fat, finely shredded cheddar cheese completes this meal beautifully.

Pork Tenderloin Tips with Stuffing and Green Beans

No need for lots of pots and pans. Do this entire meal in one easy-to-clean slow cooker.

1½ pounds pork tenderloin tips

1 tablespoon plus 1 teaspoon salt-free seasoning

2 cups hot water

1 (6-ounce) box pork- or beef-flavored stuffing, dry

1 (4-ounce) can sliced mushrooms, drained

1 small fresh onion, sliced into slivers, or ⅓ cup frozen onion slivers

1 pound frozen French-style green beans

- Spray a slow cooker with nonfat cooking spray.
- Rub the 1 tablespoon salt-free seasoning on the pork tenderloin tips and put them in a large slow cooker.
- Press an 18-inch-wide piece of heavy-duty aluminum foil, shiny side down, into a slow cooker to form a bowl. The foil bowl will be sitting on top of the pork.
- In a separate medium-size bowl mix together the hot water and dry stuffing mix along with the seasoning packet and the mushrooms. Stir until well mixed and pour into the foil bowl in the slow cooker. Fold the foil bowl closed.
- Press another 18-inch-wide piece of heavy-duty aluminum foil into the slow cooker with the shiny side of the foil facing out to form another bowl on top of the bowl holding the stuffing.
- Pour in the frozen green beans, the remaining 1 teaspoon salt-free seasoning, and the onion slivers into the top foil bowl. Fold the foil to close the bowl.
- Cover and cook on high for 5 hours or on low for 9 to 10 hours.

Yield: 6 servings (4 ounces pork, ½ cup green beans, and ½ cup stuffing per serving)

Calories: 281; Fat: 5g (17% fat); Cholesterol: 74mg; Carbohydrate: 27g; Dietary Fiber: 4g; Protein: 30g; Sodium: 635mg

 Menu idea: This is a complete meal in itself.

Sauerkraut and Pork Dinner

Even my children, who do not like sauerkraut, like this meal. It's not strong or overpowering like a lot of sauerkraut entrées.

1½ pounds pork tenderloin steaks (or buy a pork tenderloin roast and cut into 1-inch steaks)	½ cup frozen chopped onion
	1 (14-ounce) can sauerkraut
1 (16-ounce) bag fresh, baby-cut whole carrots	2 medium Granny Smith apples, chopped into tiny pieces
	1 tablespoon brown sugar

- Spray a slow cooker with nonfat cooking spray.
- Lay the meat slices on the bottom of the cooker and top with the carrots.
- In a bowl stir together the onion, sauerkraut, apples, and brown sugar.
- Pour the sauerkraut mixture over the pork and carrots.
- Cover and cook on high for 3 to 3½ hours or on low for 6 hours.

Yield: 8 (1⅓-cup) servings

Calories: 163; Fat: 4g (19% fat); Cholesterol: 55mg; Carbohydrate: 14g; Dietary Fiber: 4g; Protein: 19g; Sodium: 418mg

 Menu idea: This is a complete meal in itself. If desired, serve with rye bread and applesauce.

Sausage & Acorn Squash

To prepare this recipe faster, I mix the ingredients and fill the squash with my hands. A terrific autumn meal.

1	(14-ounce) package fat-free smoked sausage, cut into 1/4- to 1/2-inch cubes
1/4	teaspoon ground dried sage
1	tablespoon Butter Buds Sprinkles
1/3	cup packed dark brown sugar
2	acorn squash, cut in half (vertically) and cleaned out
1	cup water

- In a medium-size bowl mix the sausage, sage, Butter Buds, and brown sugar together until all of the sausage is well coated with the seasonings.
- Fill each squash heaping full with the mixture.
- Wrap each stuffed squash (4 halves total) with foil.
- Pour the water into the bottom of the slow cooker.
- Place the wrapped squash halves in the cooker. It's okay to set the squash on top of each other.
- Place the lid on the slow cooker and cook for 4 hours on high or 8 to 9 hours on low.

Yield: 4 servings (1 stuffed half squash per serving)

Calories: 262; Fat: 0g (0% fat); Cholesterol: 43mg; Carbohydrate: 52g; Dietary Fiber: 3g; Protein: 17g; Sodium: 1267mg

 Menu idea: This is good served with applesauce (cinnamon-flavored or peach-flavored would be great) and corn bread muffins.

Smothered Pork Steaks

Each succulent bite is as tasty as the one before.

4 **(4-ounce) pork tenderloin steaks (cut a I-pound tenderloin steak into 4 pieces)**	8 **ounces fresh mushrooms, sliced**
2 **large onions, quartered and separated**	¹/₄ **cup Butter Buds**
2 **large green peppers, cut into 3/4-inch strips**	¹/₂ **cup water**
	I **teaspoon celery salt or garlic salt**

- Spray a slow cooker with nonfat cooking spray.
- Place the pork tenderloin steaks in the bottom of the cooker and top with the onions, green peppers, and mushrooms.
- Mix the Butter Buds, water, and garlic salt together until the Butter Buds are dissolved. Pour over the vegetables.
- Gently toss the vegetables to distribute the seasonings.
- Cover and cook on high for 4 to 5 hours or on low for 8 to 9 hours.
- Arrange the pork steaks on a platter.
- Toss the vegetables in the juices before pouring the juice and vegetables over the pork.
- Serve hot.

Yield: 4 servings (4 ounces pork, ½ onion, ½ green pepper, and 2 ounces mushrooms per serving)

Calories: 229; Fat: 4g (16% fat); Cholesterol: 74mg; Carbohydrate: 23g; Dietary Fiber: 4g; Protein: 28g; Sodium: 660mg

 Menu idea: Served with Baked Potatoes (page 88) and Sweet Corn Bread (page 41) this is a meal combination that'll have everyone happy.

Spiced Ham Steaks

The combination of the slight sweetness and saltiness creates a terrific glaze.

3 medium-size apples, cleaned, cored, and thinly sliced with skin on	¹/₄ cup dark brown sugar
1 tablespoon Butter Buds Sprinkles	1¹/₂ teaspoons ground cinnamon
	4 (4-ounce) extra lean ham steaks

- Spray a slow cooker with nonfat cooking spray.
- In the cooker stir together the apples with the Butter Buds, brown sugar, and ground cinnamon until well mixed.
- Put the ham steaks into the cooker and coat with the mixture.
- Cover and cook on high for 2 to 3 hours or on low for 6 hours.

Yield: 4 servings

Calories: 267; Fat: 6g (20% fat); Cholesterol: 53mg; Carbohydrate: 32g; Dietary Fiber: 3g; Protein: 22g; Sodium: 1716mg

 Menu idea: The Zesty Potato Salad and the Spring Salad, both from *Busy People's Low-Fat Cookbook*, taste delicious with this entrée.

Sweet & Sour Pork

Although it's not fried, it's definitely delicious.

2	pounds pork tenderloin tips, cut into bite-size pieces	1	medium onion cut into $1/4$-inch slices, not rings
1	(20-ounce) can pineapple chunks in juice, drained	2	tablespoons flour
1	(10-ounce) jar sweet and sour sauce	5	tablespoons water

- Spray a slow cooker with nonfat cooking spray.
- In the cooker stir together the pork, pineapple, sweet and sour sauce, and onion until well mixed.
- Cover and cook on high for $3^{1}/_{2}$ to $4^{1}/_{2}$ hours or on low for 7 to 9 hours.
- Remove the meat, pineapple, and onion. In a bowl stir the flour and water together until dissolved.
- Turn the cooker to high.
- Briskly stir in the flour and water mixture.
- Cover and cook for 5 minutes or until thickened.
- Return the meat, pineapple, and onions to the sauce.

Yield: 6 (1-cup) servings

Calories: 319; Fat: 5g (15% fat); Cholesterol: 98mg; Carbohydrate: 33g; Dietary Fiber: 1g; Protein: 32g; Sodium: 250mg

★ **Sweet & Sour Chicken:** Substitute boneless, skinless chicken for the pork tenderloin.

Calories: 304; Fat: 2g (6% fat); Cholesterol: 88mg; Carbohydrate: 33g; Dietary Fiber: 1g; Protein: 36g; Sodium: 272mg

★ **Sweet & Sour Beef:** Substitute beef tenderloin for the pork tenderloin.

Calories: 374; Fat: 11g (28% fat); Cholesterol: 94mg; Carbohydrate: 33g; Dietary Fiber: 1g; Protein: 32g; Sodium: 245mg

 Menu idea: This is perfect when served with cooked rice and oriental vegetables or sugar snap peas.

Tropical Pork Dinner

This is one of my all-time favorites. I absolutely love it.

2 pounds pork tenderloin	1/4 cup apple cider vinegar
1 (20-ounce) can crushed pineapple	1/4 cup dark brown sugar
1/4 cup honey	4 large yams, washed (or 4 large sweet potatoes)

- Spray a slow cooker with nonfat cooking spray.
- Place the pork tenderloin in the cooker.
- In a bowl mix together the crushed pineapple, honey, vinegar, and brown sugar and pour over the pork.
- Place the yams on top of the meat mixture.
- Cover and cook on high for 4 1/2 to 5 1/2 hours or on low for 9 to 10 hours.
- Cut the yams in half before serving.
- If desired, pour a little sauce over the cut yams and meat.

Yield: 8 servings (4 ounces pork and 1/2 yam with 3 ounces pineapple sauce)

Calories: 318; Fat: 4g (11% fat); Cholesterol: 74mg; Carbohydrate: 47g; Dietary Fiber: 3g; Protein: 25g; Sodium: 90mg

★ **Tropical Chicken Dinner:** Substitute 8 (3-ounce) boneless, skinless chicken breasts for the pork.

Yield: 8 servings

Calories: 307; Fat: 1g (4% fat); Cholesterol: 66mg; Carbohydrate: 47g; Dietary Fiber: 3g; Protein: 28g; Sodium: 107mg

 Menu idea: This is good served with a tossed salad.

Tuna à la King

Macaroni is made of flour, liquid, and butter, as is cream sauce. The macaroni in this recipe will dissolve and make a great creamy gravy for the tasty Tuna a la King.

I	(7¼-ounce) box macaroni and cheese (Use the macaroni only. Do not make as directed.)	I	(10½-ounce) can water
3	(6-ounce) cans solid-pack white tuna	I	(10¾-ounce) can 98% fat-free cream of celery soup
I	(10½-ounce) can fat-free chicken broth	⅓	cup chopped onion
			Salt
			Pepper

- Spray a slow cooker with nonfat cooking spray.
- In the cooker gently stir together the macaroni, tuna, chicken broth, water, soup, and onion.
- Cover and cook on low for 4 to 6 hours.
- Stir the mixture until the macaroni is dissolved and becomes a thick gravy.
- Salt and pepper to taste.
- Serve over toast points or biscuits.

Note: If the gravy becomes too thick, stir in some refrigerated, fat-free, non-dairy creamer.

Yield: 4 (1-cup) servings

Calories: 394; Fat: 7g (17% fat); Cholesterol: 58mg; Carbohydrate: 39g; Dietary Fiber: 2g; Protein: 41g; Sodium: 1478mg

★ **Cheesy Tuna à la King:** Stir in the cheese packet from the box of macaroni and cheese when stirring all the ingredients together.

Calories: 426; Fat: 8g (18% fat); Cholesterol: 65mg; Carbohydrate: 42g; Dietary Fiber: 2g; Protein: 43g; Sodium: 1887mg

 Menu idea: Steamed Asparagus and the Very Berry Fruit Salad from *Busy People's Low-Fat Cookbook* complement this meal wonderfully.

Tuna Casserole

Fans of Charlie the Tuna love this.

2 **cups hot water**	1 **(15-ounce) can peas**
2 **cups elbow macaroni (Use only Mueller's brand.)**	1/2 **cup finely chopped onion**
1 **(10³/4-ounce) can 98% fat-free cream of mushroom soup**	2 **(4-ounce) cans mushroom pieces, drained**
2 **(6-ounce) cans tuna in water, not drained**	

- Spray a slow cooker with nonfat cooking spray.
- In the cooker stir together the water, macaroni, soup, tuna, peas, onion, and mushrooms until well mixed.
- Cover and cook on high for 1½ hours.

Yield: 5 (1-cup) servings

Calories: 327; Fat: 3g (8% fat); Cholesterol: 22mg; Carbohydrate: 47g; Dietary Fiber: 5g; Protein: 27g; Sodium: 958mg

★ **Cheese Tuna Casserole:** Stir in 4 ounces fat-free shredded cheddar cheese once the recipe is completely cooked.

Calories: 360; Fat: 3g (8% fat); Cholesterol: 25mg; Carbohydrate: 47g; Dietary Fiber: 5g; Protein: 33g; Sodium: 1136mg

 Menu idea: This hearty family favorite is complemented wonderfully with the Peaches and Cream Gelatin Salad and the Cucumber Dill Salad, both from *Busy People's Low-Fat Cookbook*.

Lasagna

The vegetarian sausage gives this spicy lasagna a little kick. This lasagna may be too spicy for younger children.

2 (26½-ounce) cans meat-flavored spaghetti sauce	2 (8-ounce) bags fat-free mozzarella shredded cheese
1 (12-ounce) bag vegetarian sausage crumbles (a sausage-flavored vegetarian substitute for Italian sausage)	½ cup grated Parmesan cheese
	1 (8-ounce) box uncooked lasagna (Use only Mueller's brand.)
1½ cups fat-free, small curd cottage cheese	

- Spray a slow cooker with nonfat cooking spray.
- Set aside half a can of the spaghetti sauce for after the lasagna is cooked.
- In a large bowl mix the sausage and 1½ cans of the spaghetti sauce.
- In another large bowl stir together all three cheeses until well mixed.
- Place ¾ cup of meat sauce in the bottom of the cooker. Put 2 strips of lasagna on top of the sauce. One of the strips of the lasagna will have to be broken to fill in the gaps around the unbroken piece of lasagna. Spread one-fifth of the cheese mixture over the lasagna. Place 2 strips of lasagna on the cheese. Repeat the layers three more times.
- After the last 2 strips of lasagna are used, put the last of the cheese on and then top with the meat sauce. Some cheese will show.
- Cover and cook on low for 5 to 6 hours.
- If desired, heat the reserved spaghetti sauce in the microwave until hot.
- Serve the reserved sauce on the side for anyone who wants more sauce on his serving of lasagna.

Note: For a less spicy lasagna, substitute 1 pound ground eye of round beef, browned, for the vegetarian sausage.

Yield: 10 (1-cup) servings

Calories: 309; Fat: 3g (8% fat); Cholesterol: 11mg; Carbohydrate: 35g; Dietary Fiber: 7g; Protein: 33g; Sodium: 1483mg

 Menu idea: Serve this with a tossed salad with fat-free Italian dressing and garlic toast or garlic bread.

Pizza Pasta

Expect people to ask for seconds.

2 cups hot water	2 (4-ounce) cans mushrooms, drained
1 (14-ounce) jar pizza sauce	
1/2 cup chopped onion	1 1/2 cups elbow macaroni (Use only Mueller's brand.)
2 ounces pepperoni, cut into thin strips	1/4 cup low-fat shredded mozzarella cheese

- Spray a slow cooker with nonfat cooking spray.
- In the slow cooker stir together the water, pizza sauce, onion, pepperoni, and mushrooms.
- Cover and cook on high for 1 hour.
- Add the macaroni and cook for 1/2 hour more.
- Sprinkle with the cheese.
- Cover and let cook another 10 minutes on high or until the cheese melts.

Yield: 8 (1-cup) servings

Calories: 258; Fat: 5g (18% fat); Cholesterol: 13mg; Carbohydrate: 41g; Dietary Fiber: 3g; Protein: 11g; Sodium: 919mg

★ **Vegetarian Style:** Omit the pepperoni.

Calories: 225; Fat: 2g (8% fat); Cholesterol: 7mg; Carbohydrate: 41g; Dietary Fiber: 3g; Protein: 10g; Sodium: 789mg

 Menu idea: I serve this with tossed salad and sugar-free Jell-O with light fruit cocktail for dessert.

Rigatoni

This is an Italian favorite.

1 (28-ounce) jar spaghetti sauce	1/2 cup chopped onion, optional
3 cups hot water	12 ounces rigatoni (Use only Mueller's brand.)
1 (12-ounce) bag ground meatless burger (I use Morningstar Farms.)	1 (8-ounce) container fat-free sour cream
2 (4-ounce) cans sliced mushrooms, optional	

- Spray a slow cooker with nonfat cooking spray.
- In the cooker stir together the spaghetti sauce, water, ground meatless, mushrooms, and onion, if using, until well mixed.
- Cover and cook on high for 1½ to 2 hours or on low for 3½ to 4 hours. (If cooking on low, turn to high for 10 minutes before adding rigatoni.)
- Add the rigatoni and cook for an additional ½ hour on high.
- Once fully cooked, gently stir in the sour cream and serve.

Yield: 11 (1-cup) servings

Calories: 200; Fat: 0g (0% fat); Cholesterol: 0mg; Carbohydrate: 35g; Dietary Fiber: 4g; Protein: 13g; Sodium: 352mg

 Menu idea: The Italian Dunkers from *Busy People's Low-Fat Cookbook* and a fresh green salad topped with red onion, fresh tomatoes, and fat-free Italian dressing makes a mouth-watering meal.

Sauerkraut Spaghetti

Don't let the name scare you. It is very, very good.

(32-ounce) jar low-sodium sauerkraut	tablespoon brown sugar
(26-ounce) jar spaghetti sauce	Parmesan cheese, optional

- Spray a slow cooker with nonfat cooking spray.
- Drain the sauerkraut and rinse. Squeeze dry.
- In the cooker mix together the spaghetti sauce with the sauerkraut.
- Add the brown sugar and stir.
- Cover and cook on high for 2½ hours or on low for 5 to 6 hours.
- When done, sprinkle with the grated Parmesan cheese, if desired.
- Serve warm.

Note: Calories can be cut 40 percent by using Healthy Choice Spaghetti Sauce.

Yield: 5 (1-cup) servings

Calories: 147; Fat: 1g (8% fat); Cholesterol: 0mg; Carbohydrate: 29g; Dietary Fiber: 8g; Protein: 4g; Sodium: 1104mg

 Menu idea: This is good served with a tossed salad and Garlic Toast from *Busy People's Low-Fat Cookbook*.

Spaghetti

Sauce is boss in this recipe, which is good because my children like lots of sauce.

2	(26½-ounce) jars spaghetti sauce (Hunt's or your favorite)	8	ounces spaghetti, dry and broken into 3- to 4-inch lengths (Use only Mueller's brand.)
2	cups water		

- Spray a slow cooker with nonfat cooking spray.
- Stir the spaghetti sauce and water together in slow cooker.
- Cover and cook on high for 1½ hours.
- Break the spaghetti up into thirds and put it into the sauce.
- Make sure all the pasta pieces are covered with the sauce.
- Cook on high for another ½ hour. Check to see if done; if not, cook another 5 minutes.
- Remove the spaghetti from the slow cooker and put into a serving dish.

Yield: 8 (1-cup) servings

Calories: 178; Fat: 1g (6% fat); Cholesterol: 0mg; Carbohydrate: 34g; Dietary Fiber: 5g; Protein: 7g; Sodium: 880mg

Variation: Add 1 (12-ounce) bag ground meatless burger (sausage or beef flavored).

 Menu idea: Instead of a traditional salad, serve Green Beans Italiano along with the Garlic Toast, both from *Busy People's Low-Fat Cookbook.*

Vermicelli

Some things are better left unsaid. Don't tell them this is a vegetarian meal and meat lovers will never know. Just let them love eating it.

1 (27-ounce) jar spaghetti sauce	1 (16-ounce) box vermicelli (Use only Mueller's brand.)
1 cup tomato juice	1 cup ricotta cheese
1 pound ground meatless burger (or 1 pound pre-cooked, ground eye of round beef)	8 ounces fat-free mozzarella cheese
1/2 teaspoon sage	2 tablespoons grated Parmesan cheese

- Spray a slow cooker with nonfat cooking spray.
- Set aside one cup of the spaghetti sauce. In the cooker stir together the tomato juice, ground meatless (or beef), sage, and all but the 1 cup spaghetti sauce.
- Cover and cook on high for 2 hours or on low for 4 hours.
- Stir in the vermicelli. (If cooking on low, turn the temperature to high and let sit for 5 minutes before stirring in the vermicelli.)
- Cover and cook on high for 1/2 hour.
- Stir in the ricotta cheese and the reserved 1 cup spaghetti sauce.
- Sprinkle with the mozzarella and Parmesan cheeses.
- Cover and cook on high an additional 10 minutes or until the cheese is melted.

Yield: 8 servings

Calories: 396; Fat: 3g (6% fat); Cholesterol: 12mg; Carbohydrate: 58g; Dietary Fiber: 6g; Protein: 32g; Sodium: 888mg

 Menu idea: This would be great with some garlic bread and Broccoli Parmesan from *Busy People's Low-Fat Cookbook*.

Desserts

Forbidden fruits create jams.

D esserts are my most favorite recipes to create. I absolutely love desserts. To get a smile from my family and friends I tell them, "I can't stay this sweet naturally."

I am so thrilled at the wonderful and delicious desserts I created in this slow-cooker cookbook. Most of them are unique and original as far as I know. There are also some old-time favorites I have converted from high-fat to low-fat and from a conventional oven to a slow cooker. I don't think folks would know if you didn't tell them.

Traditional-Style Cakes

This type of cake looks like a traditional cake, because the batter is cooked all together in one slow cooker. The cake itself will be only one layer. It will still be tall, and it will taste moist and delicious.

The traditional-style cake can easily be removed from the slow cooker after it has cooled for at least 10 minutes or so. During cooling time, if you have the kind of slow cooker that the crock lifts from the heating elements, I encourage you to remove the crock to promote the cooling process. If your slow cooker does not have the crock that lifts out from the slow cooker, then I encourage you to allow your cake to cool for at least 15 minutes.

To remove your cake, simply run a knife around the outside edge of the cake between the slow cooker and the cake. You may also want to gently lift the bottom edges of the cake with a long spatula to help promote loosening the cake before you turn the cake upside down onto the cake plate. It is very important that you spray the slow cooker generously with nonfat cooking spray in the beginning, before pouring the prepared batter into the slow cooker.

Be careful when turning your cake upside down onto the cake plate. The slow cookers are heavy. The face of the cake plate needs to be held very tightly and securely to the top of the slow cooker. I encourage wearing hand-mitten-style potholders. Once you have a strong hold of both the slow cooker and cake plate together, quickly invert them as you would a traditional cake pan.

As I've said, the slow cookers are heavy, so this can be difficult. You may just want to serve the cake from the slow cooker and not fuss with removing the cake from the slow cooker.

Two-Layer Cake

If you prefer having two layers of cake, simply take a piece of sewing thread or dental floss and, holding the thread with both hands, pull the thread tightly. Pull the thread through the cake as if the thread were a knife and it will separate the cake evenly across the middle into two pieces. You may need to start by gently cutting with a sharp knife an opening in the middle of the cake for the thread to begin severing through. However, I would not encourage you to cut through the entire cake with a knife, because the results are not as even as the results from using the thread. Frost the cake as you normally would if desired.

Cakes with Filling

Often the cakes will be cooked with a topping such as a cream sauce or fruit filling. It is extremely important that you be extra cautious and careful when inverting this type of cake. Only invert cakes with fruit fillings and sauces on cake plates that have at least a half-inch raised lip around the outside edge of the cake plate and only cakes that say in the recipe that they are able to be inverted. Not all of the cakes in this book can be inverted. Please read each recipe direction carefully to see whether the cake can be inverted or not when it is cooked with a fruit or cream filling. Again, this can be very difficult, so I encourage you to really think if you are physically capable of inverting the cake or not.

Spoon Cake

Spoon cakes are served directly from the slow cooker. *Do not invert spoon cakes.* This type of cake is too messy and dangerous to invert. The sauce will overflow, possibly burning you, and this will make a terrible mess.

Hot Spots

I have found that sometimes some slow cookers will have an area that cooks hotter than the rest of the slow cooker. You will know if your slow cooker has a hot spot by looking at your finished cooked cake. If there is a 3- to 4-inch area on the outer rim of your cake that is overcooked, then your slow cooker has a hot spot. Older slow cookers and less expensive brands tend to have hot spots. A hot spot is usually not a problem. However, with desserts, especially moist, tender cakes and breads, a hot spot can cause a problem for part of the dessert.

To eliminate this problem you can rotate the crock insert of your slow cooker a quarter turn every half hour to prevent your cakes from having any over cooked areas. Or with a very sharp knife you can simply cut off the small part of your cake that may have overcooked. At the very most, the amount of over cooked cake you might need to trim off would be a slight fraction of one little edge of the cake.

Almond Cake

The almond filling makes a winning frosting.

1	(12-ounce) can almond filling for pastries, cakes, and desserts	1	cup water
3	egg whites	1/3	cup applesauce
1	(18.25-ounce) box butter-flavored cake mix (I use Pillsbury.) Do not make as directed on box.	2	teaspoons almond extract

- Preheat a slow cooker to high.
- Spray the slow cooker with nonfat cooking spray.
- Spread the almond filling in the bottom of the prepared slow cooker.
- In a large bowl beat the egg whites on high speed for about 2 minutes or until soft peaks form.
- Stir in the cake mix, water, applesauce, and almond extract until well mixed. There may be some small lumps in the batter. That's okay.
- Pour the cake batter over the almond filling. Do not stir.
- Place a paper towel on top of the slow cooker. Place the slow cooker lid on top of the paper towel to cover.
- Cook on high for 1¾ hours or until a knife inserted in middle comes out clean.
- Remove the lid and the paper towel. If possible, remove the crock from the slow cooker.
- Let it cool for 15 minutes.
- Place a large serving plate with an edge (so the sauce won't overflow off the plate) upside down on top of the slow cooker. Holding the slow cooker and plate firmly together, carefully flip the cake upside down. It will be steamy hot so be *very* careful. (See page 192, Cakes with Filling.)
- Frost the sides of the cake with the almond filling from the top of the cake, leaving some almond filling on top.)
- Serve warm or chilled.

Yield: 12 servings

Calories: 279; Fat: 5g (16% fat); Cholesterol: 0mg; Carbohydrate: 55g; Dietary Fiber: 2g; Protein: 3g; Sodium: 321mg

Apple Harvest Delight

This winning dessert reminds me of a cobbler and an apple crumb pie without the crust. Beware, it is rich and a little bit goes a long way.

1 teaspoon ground cinnamon	1 (18.25-ounce) box French vanilla cake mix (I use Pillsbury Moist Supreme.) Do not make as directed on box.
1/2 teaspoon ground cloves	
1 cup quick-cooking oats (I use Quaker.)	1 (21-ounce) can cinnamon spice apple pie filling

- Preheat a slow cooker on high for 10 minutes.
- Spray the cooker with nonfat cooking spray.
- In a large bowl stir together the dry cake mix, cinnamon, cloves, and dry oats until well mixed.
- Insert a sharp knife into an opened can of apple pie filling and cut the apples into small pieces.
- Spread 1 cup of the dry cake mixture on bottom of slow cooker.
- Spread half the can of apple pie filling over the dry cake mix.
- Spread 2 cups of the dry cake mixture over the pie filling.
- Spread the remaining pie filling over the second layer of dry cake mixture.
- Spread the remaining dry cake mixture over the pie filling.
- Spray the top with nonfat cooking spray.
- Cover and cook on high for 2 hours.
- Serve directly from the slow cooker. *Do not invert.*

Yield: 15 (1/2-cup) servings

Calories: 206; Fat: 4g (16% fat); Cholesterol: 0mg; Carbohydrate: 41g; Dietary Fiber: 2g; Protein: 3g; Sodium: 234mg

Brownies

I use a large oblong slow cooker to make these. I was surprised to test this recipe and find out these brownies cook great in the slow cooker. No special ingredients, but the fact we can make brownies in a slow cooker is great when you're in a pinch and your oven is already in use.

1 (10.25-ounce) package fudge brownie mix (I use Betty Crocker.) Do not make as directed on package.	2 tablespoons water
	1/4 cup applesauce
	2 egg whites

- Preheat a slow cooker to high.
- Spray the cooker with nonfat cooking spray.
- In a medium-size bowl stir together the brownie mix, water, applesauce, and egg whites until well mixed.
- Pour the mixture into the prepared slow cooker.
- Cover and cook on high for 1 hour.
- Remove the crock from the cooker.
- Remove the lid and let it cool for 10 minutes.
- If you wish to invert the brownies, please read Traditional-Style Cakes on page 191 about removing traditional cakes.

Yield: 9 brownies

Calories: 141; Fat: 4g (22% fat); Cholesterol: 1mg; Carbohydrate: 26g; Dietary Fiber: 1g; Protein: 3g; Sodium: 138mg

Bread Pudding

This was one of my favorite old-fashioned comfort foods that I was unable to enjoy very often because it was too high in calories and fat, but now I can enjoy every tasty bite totally guilt free whenever I want.

4 egg whites	$1/2$ cup fat-free French vanilla nondairy liquid creamer
$1/4$ cup Splenda (measures like sugar)	4 cups French bread, cut into $1/2$-inch cubes
$1/2$ teaspoon ground cinnamon	$1/4$ cup dried cranberries (or raisins)
$1/2$ cup skim milk	

- Preheat a slow cooker to high.
- Spray the slow cooker with non-fat cooking spray.
- In a bowl stir the egg whites, Splenda, cinnamon, milk, and creamer together until well mixed.
- Gently stir in to the bowl the bread cubes and dried cranberries (or raisins) until well saturated with egg mixture.
- Spread the mixture in the bottom of the slow cooker.
- Cook on high for 1¾ to 2 hours or until a knife inserted in the middle of the bread pudding comes out clean.
- Remove the crock from the slow cooker. Remove the lid.
- Serve hot or chilled directly from slow cooker.

Yield: 6 (½ cup) servings

Calories: 142; Fat: 1g (7% fat); Cholesterol: 1mg; Carbohydrate: 26g; Dietary Fiber: 1g; Protein: 5g; Sodium: 191mg

Carrot Cake

Even Bugs Bunny would be impressed with how super moist this carrot cake is.

6 egg whites	1 (18.25–ounce) box carrot cake
1/2 cup fat-free sour cream	mix, dry (I use Betty Crocker
1/2 cup applesauce	Super Moist.) Do not make as
1 teaspoon ground cinnamon	directed on box.
	1/4 cup finely chopped walnuts
	3 cups finely shredded carrots

- Preheat a slow cooker to high.
- Spray the slow cooker with nonfat cooking spray.
- In a mixing bowl with a mixer on medium speed beat the egg whites, sour cream, applesauce, cinnamon and cake mix together for two minutes, scraping the sides of the bowl occasionally.
- With the spatula stir into the batter the walnuts and carrots until well mixed.
- Pour the prepared cake batter into the slow cooker.
- Place a paper towel on top of the slow cooker. Place the lid of the slow cooker on the paper towel.
- Cook on high for 1½ to 1¾ hours or until a knife inserted in the middle of the cake comes out clean.
- Remove the crock from the slow cooker. Remove the lid and the paper towel, and let it cool for 10 to 15 minutes.
- Run a knife around the outside edge of the cake to loosen it from the slow cooker.
- Place a large serving plate upside down on the top of the slow cooker. Holding the slow cooker and the plate firmly together, carefully flip the cake upside down. It will be steamy hot so be very careful. (See page 192, Cakes with Filling.)
- Serve hot or chilled.

Yield: 12 servings

Calories: 234; Fat: 6g (22% fat); Cholesterol: 2mg; Carbohydrate: 41g; Dietary Fiber: 2g; Protein: 5g; Sodium: 316mg

Maple Snack Cake

This is very versatile. It's good for breakfast instead of toast or as a moist snack cake anytime of the day.

³/₄ cup light maple syrup

2 tablespoons applesauce

8 egg whites (or I cup Egg Beaters)

I (18.25-ounce) box cake mix (I use Betty Crocker Super Moist.) Do not make as directed on box.

- Preheat a slow cooker 10 minutes on high.
- Spray the cooker with nonfat cooking spray.
- In a bowl briskly mix together the maple syrup, applesauce, egg whites, and cake mix for 2 minutes.
- Pour the mixture into the prepared cooker.
- Place a paper towel on top of the slow cooker.
- Place the lid of the cooker on the paper towel to cover.
- Cook on high for 2 hours.
- Place a large serving plate with an edge upside down on top of the slow cooker. Holding the slow cooker and plate firmly together, carefully flip the cake upside down. It will be steamy hot so be *very* careful.
- Let the cake cool 10 minutes.

Note: You may want to serve this dessert with a spoon from the slow cooker if you are concerned about inverting the cake.

Yield: 12 servings

Calories: 338; Fat: 2g (8% fat); Cholesterol: 0mg; Carbohydrate: 74g; Dietary Fiber: 0g; Protein: 8g; Sodium: 592mg

Marshmallow Applesauce Dessert

Cooking this recipe in the slow cooker allows the oven to be free for other uses.

4 cups applesauce	2 cups mini marshmallows (or quartered regular marshmallows)
¼ teaspoon allspice	
½ teaspoon cinnamon	

- Spray a slow cooker with nonfat cooking spray.
- In the cooker mix the applesauce, allspice, and cinnamon together.
- Sprinkle the marshmallows on top.
- Cook on low for 3 to 4 hours or on high for 1½ to 2 hours.
- Serve warm. *Do not invert this dessert.* Serve directly from the slow cooker.
- Refrigerate any unused portions.

Yield: 15 servings

Calories: 48; Fat: 0g (0% fat); Cholesterol: 0mg; Carbohydrate: 12g; Dietary Fiber: 1g; Protein: 0g; Sodium: 4mg

Pistachio-Nut Snack Cake

Very moist and flavorful. I like it warm with low-fat frozen yogurt.

1 cup applesauce 8 egg whites 1 cup water 2 (3.4-ounce) boxes instant pistachio pudding	1 (18.25-ounce) box yellow cake mix, dry (I use Betty Crocker Super Moist with pudding in the mix.) Fat-free whipped topping or low-fat frozen yogurt, optional

- Preheat the slow cooker to high.
- Spray the slow cooker with nonfat cooking spray.
- In a medium-size mixing bowl mix the applesauce, egg whites, water, pudding, and cake mix together for 2 minutes.
- Pour the mixture into the prepared cooker.
- Place a paper towel over the slow cooker. Put the lid of the cooker on the paper towel to cover.
- Cook on high for 1½ to 2 hours or until a toothpick inserted in the center of the cake comes out clean.
- Remove the lid and paper towel. Remove the crock from the cooker, and let it cool for 10 minutes.
- Place a large serving plate with an edge upside down on top of the slow cooker. Holding the slow cooker and plate firmly together, carefully flip the cake upside down. It will be steamy hot so be *very* careful. (See page 191, Traditional-Style Cakes.)
- If desired, serve with a dab of whipped topping or low-fat frozen yogurt.
- Refrigerate any unused portions.

Yield: 15 servings

Calories: 210; Fat: 3g (13% fat); Cholesterol: 0mg; Carbohydrate: 42g; Dietary Fiber: 0g; Protein: 3g; Sodium: 441mg

Pumpkin Cake

This cake is best not frosted *and served warm with whipped topping.*

4 egg whites	1 (16-ounce) can pumpkin
²/₃ cup light brown sugar	1 (18.25-ounce) box light yellow
¹/₃ cup sugar	cake mix (I use Betty Crocker
1 teaspoon ground cinnamon	Super Moist.)
¹/₂ teaspoon allspice	

- Preheat the cooker for 10 minutes on high.
- Spray a slow cooker with nonfat cooking spray.
- Mix the egg whites, brown sugar, sugar, cinnamon, allspice, pumpkin, and cake mix together and pour into the preheated slow cooker.
- Cover the top of the slow cooker with a paper towel under the lid or leave the top slightly ajar.
- Cook for 1½ hours on high or until toothpick inserted in center comes out clean.
- Remove the lid and paper towel. Remove the crock from the slow cooker, and let it cool for 10 minutes.
- Place a large serving plate with an edge upside down on top of the slow cooker. Holding the slow cooker and plate firmly together, carefully flip the cake upside down. (See page 191, Traditional-Style Cakes.)

Yield: 15 servings

Calories: 199; Fat: 1g (4% fat); Cholesterol: 0mg; Carbohydrate: 47g; Dietary Fiber: 1g; Protein: 3g; Sodium: 247mg

Sour Cream Chocolate Cake

This is a moist and delicious cake.

1 (18.25-ounce) devil's food cake mix, dry (I use Betty Crocker Super Moist.) Do not make as directed on box. 6 egg whites	1/2 cup fat-free sour cream 3/4 cup cold water Fat-free whipped topping, optional

- Preheat the cooker on high for 10 minutes.
- Spray a slow cooker with nonfat cooking spray.
- In the cooker stir together the cake mix, egg whites, sour cream, and water until well mixed.
- Pour the mixture into the prepared slow cooker.
- Place a paper towel over the top of the slow cooker and cover with the cooker lid.
- Cook on high for 1½ hours or until toothpick inserted in center comes out clean.
- Remove the lid and paper towel. Remove the crock from the slow cooker, and let it cool for 15 minutes.
- Place a large serving plate with an edge upside down on top of the slow cooker. Holding the slow cooker and plate firmly together, carefully flip the cake upside down. It will be steamy hot so be *very* careful. (See page 191, Traditional-Style Cakes.)
- Serve with a dab of fat-free whipped topping, if desired.

Note: You may want to serve this dessert with a spoon from the slow cooker if you are concerned about inverting the cake.

Yield: 12 (½-cup) servings

Calories: 201; Fat: 4g (19% fat); Cholesterol: 0mg; Carbohydrate: 35g; Dietary Fiber: 1g; Protein: 4g; Sodium: 367mg

Strawberry Shortcake

There's nothing like homemade strawberry shortcake with fresh, sweet strawberries and whipped cream. Mmmmm.

2¼ cups reduced-fat pancake mix (I use Bisquick.)	3 tablespoons applesauce
3 tablespoons no-calorie sweetener (I use Splenda. Use the kind that measures like sugar.)	1 quart fresh strawberries cleaned and sliced, about 2 pounds
⅔ cup skim milk	8 tablespoons fat-free whipped topping

- Preheat a slow cooker to high and spray with nonfat cooking spray.
- In a bowl mix together the pancake mix, Splenda, milk, and applesauce until it forms a ball of dough.
- Press the dough into the bottom of the cooker with your hands as you would pizza dough, making sure to cover the entire bottom of the slow cooker.
- Cover and cook on high for 1¼ hours or until a toothpick inserted in the middle comes out clean.
- While the shortcake is cooking, in a bowl gently sprinkle the sweetener or sugar to taste onto the strawberry slices, coating the berries evenly.
- Once the shortcake is cooked, immediately remove the cake from the cooker by gently loosening it with a spatula. Once the cake is completely loosened turn the cooker upside down. The cake should come out easily.
- Place a serving plate on the bottom of the cake (the bottom is facing upward now). Slide a large spatula under the cake and flip the cake right side up.
- Put one-eighth of the strawberries on each serving of shortcake.
- Top the berries with 1 tablespoon whipped topping.

Yield: 8 servings

Calories: 167; Fat: 2g (12% fat); Cholesterol: 0mg; Carbohydrate: 35g; Dietary Fiber: 2g; Protein: 4g; Sodium: 406mg

Apple Spice Upside-Down Cake

For an extra treat serve with fat-free vanilla ice cream or whipped topping.

6 egg whites	1/2 plus 1/2 teaspoon ground cinnamon
1/2 cup apple butter	
1 cup water	1/2 plus 1/2 teaspoon ground allspice
1 (18.25-ounce) box yellow cake mix, dry (I use Betty Crocker Super Moist.) Do not make as directed on box.	1 (20-ounce) can apple pie filling

- Preheat a slow cooker to high.
- Spray the cooker with nonfat cooking spray.
- In a large bowl with a hand mixer on high speed, beat the egg whites, apple butter, and water until foamy.
- Add the cake mix, $\frac{1}{2}$ teaspoon ground cinnamon, and $\frac{1}{2}$ teaspoon ground allspice. Reduce the speed to medium and mix for another minute.
- In a medium size bowl stir together the apple pie filling, the remaining $\frac{1}{2}$ teaspoon ground cinnamon, and the remaining $\frac{1}{2}$ teaspoon ground allspice until well mixed.
- Spread the pie filling on the bottom of the prepared slow cooker.
- Pour the cake batter over the pie filling. Do not stir.
- Place a paper towel on top of the slow cooker and cover with the lid.
- Cook on high for 2 to $2\frac{1}{2}$ hours or until knife inserted in center comes out clean.
- Turn the slow cooker off and let it sit for 10 minutes.
- Remove the lid and paper towel. Run a knife along the edge of the slow cooker to loosen the cake.
- Place a large serving plate with an edge (so the sauce won't overflow off the plate) upside down on top of the slow cooker. Holding the slow cooker and plate firmly together, carefully flip the cake upside down. It will be steamy hot so be *very* careful. The apple pie filling will ooze down the sides of the cake. (See page 192, Cakes with Filling.)

Yield: 12 servings

Calories: 256; Fat: 4g (12% fat); Cholesterol: 0mg; Carbohydrate: 53g; Dietary Fiber: 1g; Protein: 4g; Sodium: 339mg

Banana Cream Upside-Down Cake

Scrumptious!

3 egg whites	1 (3^1/2-ounce) box banana cream, cook-and-serve pudding mix, dry—Do not make as directed on box.
2 medium bananas, smashed to equal 1 cup	
^{1}/2 plus 2 cups water	
1 (18.25-ounce) box yellow cake mix—Do not make as directed on box.	

- Preheat a slow cooker on high.
- Spray the cooker with nonfat cooking spray.
- In a large bowl beat the egg whites with a mixer on high speed until soft peaks form, about 1 to 2 minutes.
- In a separate bowl, put the bananas. With the mixer beat on high until the bananas are puréed.
- Put 1 cup of the bananas in with the egg whites. (Discard any extra bananas).
- Add the ^{1}/2 cup water and the dry cake mix to the eggs and bananas. With the mixer beat together for about 1 to 2 minutes, scraping the sides of the bowl occasionally. The batter will be thick.
- In the prepared slow cooker stir together the dry pudding mix and the remaining 2 cups of water. Stir until completely dissolved.
- Pour the prepared cake batter and the pudding into the slow cooker. *Do not stir.*
- Place a paper towel on top of the slow cooker. Place the lid of the slow cooker on the paper towel to cover.
- Cook on high for 2 hours.
- Place a large serving plate with an edge (so the sauce won't overflow off the plate) upside down on top of the slow cooker. Holding the slow cooker and plate firmly together, carefully flip the cake upside down. It will be steamy hot so be *very* careful. The sauce will ooze down the sides of the cake. (See page 192, Cakes with Filling.)

Yield: 12 servings

Calories: 227; Fat: 4g (14% fat); Cholesterol: 0mg; Carbohydrate: 46g; Dietary Fiber: 0g; Protein: 3g; Sodium: 359mg

Blueberry Upside-Down Cake

Home run. Yes, sir. I hit a home run when I created this winner. Absolutely delicious and oh, so pretty.

6	egg whites	1	(21-ounce) can blueberry pie filling
1	cup water		Fat-free whipped topping, optional
1/3	cup applesauce		
1	(18.25-ounce) box French vanilla cake mix, dry (I use Betty Crocker Super Moist.) Do not make as directed on box.		

- Preheat a slow cooker to high.
- Spray the cooker with nonfat cooking spray.
- In a large bowl beat the egg whites on high speed with a mixer for 1 to 2 minutes or until soft peaks form.
- Reduce the speed to medium and mix in the water, applesauce, and cake mix. Mix for another minute, scraping the sides of the bowl often.
- Pour the pie filling into the bottom of the prepared slow cooker.
- Pour the cake batter over the pie filling. Do not stir.
- Place a paper towel on top of the slow cooker and put the lid on the paper towel to cover.
- Cook on high for 2 hours.
- Take the lid and paper towel off.
- Take the crock out of the slow cooker (if possible).
- Let it cool for 10 minutes.
- Place a large serving plate with an edge (so the sauce won't overflow off the plate) upside down on top of the slow cooker. Holding the slow cooker and plate firmly together, carefully flip the cake upside down. It will be steamy hot so be *very* careful. The berries will ooze down the sides of the cake. (See page 192, Cakes with Filling.)
- Serve hot, chilled, or at room temperature with fat-free whipped topping, if desired.

Yield: 12 servings

Calories: 243; Fat: 4g (15% fat); Cholesterol: 0mg; Carbohydrate: 48g; Dietary Fiber: 2g; Protein: 4g; Sodium: 311mg

Black Forest Upside-Down Cake

I'm so very, very excited about this cake. It looks beautiful and is very impressive. Tastes great.

6 egg whites

$^1/_2$ cup applesauce

1 cup water

1 (18.25-ounce) chocolate cake mix, dry (I use Betty Crocker Super Moist Butter Recipe.) Do not make as directed on box.

1 (20-ounce) can light cherry pie filling

Fat-free whipped topping optional

- Preheat a slow cooker on high.
- Spray the slow cooker with nonfat cooking spray.
- In a large mixing bowl with a hand mixer beat the egg whites, applesauce, and water together on medium speed until soft peaks form.
- Gently fold the cake mix into the peaks.
- Pour the pie filling into the bottom of the cooker.
- Pour the batter over the pie filling. Do not stir.
- Place the paper towel on top of the slow cooker and place the lid over the paper towel to cover. Cook on high for 2 hours or until a knife inserted in center comes out clean.
- Turn off the cooker. If possible, take the crock out of slow cooker. Remove the lid and paper towel. Let it sit for 10 minutes. Run a knife along edge of the slow cooker to loosen the cake.
- Place a large serving plate with an edge (so the sauce won't overflow off the plate) upside down on top of the slow cooker. Holding the slow cooker and plate firmly together, carefully flip the cake upside down. It will be steamy hot so be *very* careful. (See page 192, Cakes with Filling.)
- If desired, serve with fat-free whipped topping or fat-free vanilla ice cream. Good served hot, cold, or at room temperature.

Yield: 12 servings

Calories: 213; Fat: 4g (17% fat); Cholesterol: 0mg; Carbohydrate: 39g; Dietary Fiber: 2g; Protein: 4g; Sodium: 364mg

Butterscotch Cream Upside-Down Cake

This is tasty whether served hot or chilled.

3 egg whites	(comes in 3¹/₂-ounce boxes) Do not make as directed on box.
¹/₃ cup applesauce	
1¹/₄ plus 2 cups water	1 (18.25-ounce) box white cake mix, dry (I use Betty Crocker Super Moist.) Do not make as directed on box.
1 ounce plus 3¹/₂ ounces butterscotch-flavored, cook-and-serve pudding mix, dry	

- Preheat a slow cooker to high.
- Spray the slow cooker with nonfat cooking spray.
- Beat the egg whites with a mixer on high until soft peaks form.
- Add the applesauce, 1¹/₄ cups water, 1 ounce of the pudding mix, and the cake mix. Continue beating on medium with mixer for 2 minutes longer, scraping the sides of the bowl occasionally.
- In the prepared slow cooker stir together the remaining 3¹/₂ ounces (1 box) of the pudding mix and 2 cups of water. Stir until completely dissolved.
- Pour the prepared cake mix into the prepared pudding mixture in the slow cooker. Do not stir.
- Place a paper towel on top of the slow cooker. Cover by placing the lid of the slow cooker on the paper towel.
- Cook on high for 2 hours. Unplug the slow cooker (and if possible, remove the crock from the slow cooker.) Remove the lid and paper towel, and let it cool for 10 minutes.
- Run a knife around the edge of the cake to loosen it from the slow cooker.
- Place a large serving plate with an edge (so the sauce won't overflow off the plate) upside down on top of the slow cooker. Holding the slow cooker and plate firmly together, carefully flip the cake upside down. It will be steamy hot so be *very* careful. The sauce will ooze down the sides of the cake. (See page 192, Cakes with Filling.)
- Serve hot or chilled.

Yield: 12 servings

Calories: 247; Fat: 4g (15% fat); Cholesterol: 0mg; Carbohydrate: 50g; Dietary Fiber: 1g; Protein: 3g; Sodium: 370mg

Cherry Upside-Down Cake

If every cake could be as easy to prepare as this moist, delicious, beauty the bakery would have a hard time selling their cakes.

6 egg whites	Super Moist.) Do not make as directed in box.
1/2 cup applesauce	
1 cup water	1 (21-ounce) can light cherry pie filling
1 (18.25-ounce) box yellow cake mix, dry (I use Betty Crocker	

- Preheat slow cooker to high.
- Spray the slow cooker with non-fat cooking spray.
- In a mixing bowl with a mixer on medium speed beat the egg whites, applesauce, water, and cake mix together for two minutes, scraping the sides of the bowl occasionally.
- Spread the pie filling in the bottom of the slow cooker.
- Pour the prepared cake batter on top of the pie filling.
- Place a paper towel on top of the slow cooker. Place the lid of the slow cooker on the paper towel.
- Cook on high for 1¾ to 2 hours or until a knife inserted in the middle of the cake comes out clean.
- Remove the crock from the slow cooker. Remove the lid and the paper towel, and let it cool for 10 to 15 minutes.
- Run a knife around the outside edge of the cake to loosen it from the slow cooker.
- Place a large serving plate with an edge (so the pie filling won't overflow off the plate) upside down on the top of the slow cooker. Holding the slow cooker and the plate firmly together, carefully flip the cake upside down. It will be steamy hot so be very careful. The pie filling will ooze down the sides of the cake. (See page 192, Cakes with Filling.)
- Serve hot or chilled.

Yield: 12 servings

Calories: 211; Fat: 4g (15% fat); Cholesterol: 0mg; Carbohydrate: 41g; Dietary Fiber: 1g; Protein: 3g; Sodium: 323mg

Coconut Cream Upside-Down Cake

If you like coconut cream pie and coconut cake you'll love this. I love it warm.

1	plus 1 (3-ounce) boxes coconut-flavored, cook-and-serve pudding	$^1/_3$	cup applesauce
2	plus 1$^1/_4$ cups hot water	1	(18.25-ounce) box white cake mix, dry (I use Betty Crocker Super Moist.) Do not make as directed on box.
3	egg whites		

- Preheat a slow cooker to high.
- Spray the cooker with nonfat cooking spray.
- In the prepared slow cooker with a hand mixer on high, mix together 1 box of pudding mix and 2 cups of water for 1 minute.
- Put the lid on the slow cooker.
- In a large bowl beat the egg whites on high until foamy.
- Add the remaining box of pudding mix and 1$^1/_4$ cups water along with applesauce and the cake mix, and beat on medium for 1 minute longer.
- Pour the cake mixture in the slow cooker. *Do not stir.*
- Place a paper towel on top of the slow cooker. Place the lid of the slow cooker on the paper towel to cover.
- Cook on high for 2 to 2$^1/_2$ hours or until a toothpick inserted in the middle comes out clean. Remove the lid and the paper towel.
- Turn off the slow cooker. If possible, remove the crock from the slow cooker and let it cool for 10 minutes.
- Place a large serving plate with an edge (so the sauce won't overflow off the plate) upside down on top of the slow cooker. Holding the slow cooker and plate firmly together, carefully flip the cake upside down. It will be steamy hot so be *very* careful. The sauce will ooze down the sides of the cake. (See page 192, Cakes with Filling.)
- Let the cake cool for 5 minutes before serving. The coconut cream sauce will firm as it cools. Serve hot or chilled. Refrigerate uneaten portions.

Yield: 12 servings

Calories: 245; Fat: 5g (18% fat); Cholesterol: 0mg; Carbohydrate: 47g; Dietary Fiber: 1g; Protein: 3g; Sodium: 435mg

Lemon Blueberry Upside-Down Cake

Two thumbs up for this mouth-watering combination.

1 **(21-ounce) can blueberry pie filling**	**Pillsbury.) Do not make as directed on box.**
3 **egg whites**	1 **cup water**
1 **(18.25-ounce) box lemon-flavored cake mix, dry (I use**	1/3 **cup applesauce**

- Preheat a slow cooker to high.
- Spray the cooker with nonfat cooking spray.
- Spread the blueberry pie filling on the bottom of the prepared cooker.
- In a large bowl beat the egg whites with a mixer on high speed for about 2 minutes or until soft peaks form.
- Stir in the cake mix, water, and applesauce. Continue stirring until well mixed. Some small lumps in the batter are okay.
- Pour the batter on top of the blueberry pie filling in the slow cooker. Do not stir.
- Place a paper towel on top of the slow cooker. Cover by placing the lid of the slow cooker on the paper towel.
- Cook on high for 2 hours or until a toothpick inserted in the middle comes out clean.
- Unplug the slow cooker, and if possible, remove the crock from the slow cooker. Remove the lid and the paper towel, and let it cool for 15 minutes.
- Place a large serving plate with an edge (so the sauce won't overflow off the plate) upside down on top of the slow cooker. Holding the slow cooker and plate firmly together, carefully flip the cake upside down. It will be steamy hot so be *very* careful. The berries will ooze down the sides of the cake. (See page 192, Cakes with Filling.)

Note: If desired you can spoon this cake out of the slow cooker instead of removing the cake.

Yield: 12 servings

Calories: 233; Fat: 3g (13% fat); Cholesterol: 0mg; Carbohydrate: 49g; Dietary Fiber: 2g; Protein: 3g; Sodium: 300mg

Peach Upside-Down Cake

The flavorful aroma of this cake while it is cooking makes the whole house smell cozy and inviting.

6 egg whites	1 (18.25-ounce) box yellow cake mix, dry (I use Betty Crocker Super Moist.) Do not make as directed in box.
¹/₂ cup applesauce	
1 cup water	
1 teaspoon ground cinnamon	
¹/₂ teaspoon ground allspice	1 (21-ounce) can peach pie filling

- Preheat slow cooker to high.
- Spray the slow cooker with non-fat cooking spray.
- In a mixing bowl with a mixer on medium speed beat the egg whites, applesauce, water, cinnamon, allspice and cake mix together for two minutes, scraping the sides of the bowl occasionally.
- Spread the pie filling in the bottom of the slow cooker.
- Pour the prepared cake batter on top of the pie filling.
- Place a paper towel on top of the slow cooker. Place the lid of the slow cooker on the paper towel.
- Cook on high for 1¾ to 2 hours or until a knife inserted in the middle of the cake comes out clean.
- Remove the crock from the slow cooker. Remove the lid and the paper towel, and let it cool for 10 to 15 minutes.
- Run a knife around the outside edge of the cake to loosen it from the slow cooker.
- Place a large serving plate with an edge (so the pie filling won't overflow off the plate) upside down on the top of the slow cooker. Holding the slow cooker and the plate firmly together, carefully flip the cake upside down. It will be steamy hot so be very careful. The pie filling will ooze down the sides of the cake. (See page 192, Cakes with Filling.)
- Serve hot or chilled.

Yield: 12 servings

Calories: 236; Fat: 4g (13% fat); Cholesterol: 0mg; Carbohydrate: 47g; Dietary Fiber: 1g; Protein: 4g; Sodium: 326mg

Raspberry Upside-Down Cake

Mmm, Mmm, good!

3 egg whites	1 (18.25-ounce) box cherry-chip-flavored cake mix (I use Betty Crocker Super Moist.) Do not make as directed on box.
1¼ cups water	
⅓ cup applesauce	
1 (3-ounce) box sugar-free raspberry gelatin (I use Jell-O.) Do not make as directed on box.	1 (12-ounce) can red raspberry filling (I use Solo.)

- Preheat a slow cooker to high.
- Spray the cooker with nonfat cooking spray.
- In a large bowl beat the egg whites with an electric mixer on high speed for 1 to 2 minutes or until soft peaks form.
- To the beaten eggs add the water, applesauce, gelatin mix, and cake mix. Beat on medium speed with the mixer for 2 minutes, scraping the bowl occasionally.
- Spread the red raspberry filling in the bottom of the prepared slow cooker.
- Pour the prepared batter over the red raspberry filling in the slow cooker. Do not stir.
- Place a paper towel on top of the slow cooker. Place the lid of the slow cooker on the paper towel to cover.
- Cook on high for 2 hours.
- Remove the crock from the cooker. Take off the lid and paper towel, and let it cool for 15 minutes.
- Place a large serving plate with an edge (so the sauce won't overflow off the plate) upside down on top of the slow cooker. Holding the slow cooker and plate firmly together, carefully flip the cake upside down. It will be steamy hot so be *very* careful. The berries will ooze down the sides of the cake. (See page 192, Cakes with Filling.)

Note: You may want to serve this dessert with a spoon from the slow cooker if you are concerned about inverting the cake.

Yield: 12 servings

Calories: 222; Fat: 5g (21% fat); Cholesterol: 11mg; Carbohydrate: 40g; Dietary Fiber: 1g; Protein: 4g; Sodium: 360mg

Very Vanilla Upside-Down Cake with Vanilla Cream

Super moist.

2½ plus 1½ cups water	1 (18.25-ounce) box white cake mix, dry (I use Betty Crocker Super Moist.) Do not make as directed on box.
1 (4.6-ounce) box vanilla-flavored cook-and-serve pudding mix, dry—Do not make as directed on box.	
3 egg whites	2 teaspoons vanilla
	⅓ cup applesauce

- Preheat a slow cooker on high.
- Spray the slow cooker with nonfat cooking spray.
- Stir the 2½ cups water and the pudding mix in the prepared slow cooker until dissolved and cover.
- In a large bowl beat the egg whites with a mixer on high until foamy.
- Stir in the cake mix, vanilla, applesauce, and the remaining 1½ cups water. Stir for 2 minutes. The batter will be lumpy.
- Pour the batter into the pudding mixture in the slow cooker. Do not stir.
- Place a paper towel on top of the slow cooker. Cover by placing the lid of the slow cooker on the paper towel.
- Cook on high for 2 hours. Remove the lid and the paper towel. Unplug the slow cooker, and if possible, remove the crock from the slow cooker. Let it sit for 10 minutes.
- Run a knife around the edge of the cake to loosen from the slow cooker.
- Place a large serving plate with an edge (so the sauce won't overflow off the plate) upside down on top of the slow cooker. Holding the slow cooker and plate firmly together, carefully flip the cake upside down. It will be steamy hot so be *very* careful. The sauce will ooze down the sides of the cake. (See page 192, Cakes with Filling.)
- Serve hot or chilled.

Yield: 12 servings

Calories: 231; Fat: 4g (16% fat); Cholesterol: 0mg; Carbohydrate: 45g; Dietary Fiber: 1g; Protein: 3g; Sodium: 354mg

Apricot Spoon Cake

Always delightful.

Cake:
- 1 (17-ounce) can apricot halves in heavy syrup
- 1 (18.25-ounce) yellow cake mix, dry (I use Betty Crocker Super Moist.)

Frosting:
- 1 cup apricot preserves, divided
- 1 (1-ounce) box sugar-free, instant vanilla pudding and pie filling, dry
- 1 (12-ounce) container fat-free whipped topping

- Preheat a slow cooker on high for 10 minutes.
- Spray the slow cooker with nonfat cooking spray.
- In a blender, purée the apricots with the heavy syrup until smooth and thick.
- In a medium bowl using a mixer, combine the dry cake mix and puréed apricots on medium speed for 2 minutes.
- Pour the mixture into the cooker.
- Place a paper towel over the cooker. Put the lid of the cooker on top of the paper towel to cover.
- Cook on high for 2½ hours or until a toothpick inserted in the center comes out clean.
- To make the frosting, in a medium bowl using a mixer, stir together the apricot preserves with the dry pudding mix and whipped topping. Mix on low for about 1 minute or until well mixed.
- Serve from the slow cooker. *Do not invert this dessert.* (For information on spoon cakes and spoon desserts please read page 193.)
- Refrigerate any leftover cake.

Yield: 15 servings

Calories: 257; Fat: 1g (3% fat); Cholesterol: 0mg; Carbohydrate: 61g; Dietary Fiber: 1g; Protein: 2g; Sodium: 288mg

Black Forest Spoon Dessert

Prepare, stir, cook, and serve this dish all from one slow cooker. It's absolutely delicious on cold, blistery days, and cleanup could not be easier; there's no bowl to wash.

1	(20-ounce) can light cherry pie filling
1	(18.25-ounce) box chocolate cake mix, butter recipe (I use Betty Crocker Super Moist.) Do not make as directed on box.

- Preheat a slow cooker to high for 10 minutes.
- Spray the cooker with nonfat cooking spray.
- In the cooker stir together the pie filling and cake mix until there is no dry cake mix visible. The batter will be very thick and lumpy.
- Place a paper towel on top of the slow cooker.
- Put the slow cooker lid on the paper towel.
- Cook on high for 2 to 2¼ hours or until a knife inserted in the center comes out clean.
- Serve directly from the cooker. *Do not invert this cake.*

Yield: 15 (½-cup) servings

Calories: 160; Fat: 3g (8% fat); Cholesterol: 0mg; Carbohydrate: 32g; Dietary Fiber: 1g; Protein: 2g; Sodium: 221mg

Blueberry Cobbler Spoon Dessert

So rich and filling. A little serving goes a long way.

I (18.25-ounce) French vanilla cake mix, dry (I use Betty Crocker Super Moist.) Do not make as directed on box.	I (21-ounce) can blueberry pie filling Fat-free whipped topping, optional

- Spray a slow cooker with nonfat cooking spray.
- Set ⅓ cup of the dry cake mix aside.
- Sprinkle half of the remaining dry cake mix in the bottom of slow cooker.
- Spread half the can of blueberry pie filling over the dry cake mix.
- Repeat the layers until the ingredients are used up.
- Sprinkle the ⅓ cup of dry cake mix that was previously set aside on top of the pie filling.
- Cover and cook on high for 2 hours.
- Serve hot with a dab of whipped topping, if desired. *Do not invert this dessert.* Serve directly from the slow cooker. (For information on spoon cakes and spoon desserts please read page 193.)

Yield: 12 (3-ounce) servings

Calories: 232; Fat: 4g (16% fat); Cholesterol: 0mg; Carbohydrate: 47g; Dietary Fiber: 2g; Protein: 2g; Sodium: 284mg

Blueberry Delight Spoon Dessert

Very rich. Very great.

$^3/_4$ cup oatmeal (I use Quaker Quick Oats), dry	1 (20-ounce) can blueberry pie filling
1 (18.25-ounce) box vanilla cake mix with pudding in the mix (I use Betty Crocker Super Moist.)	

- Preheat a slow cooker for 10 minutes on high.
- Spray the cooker with nonfat cooking spray.
- In a large bowl mix together the oatmeal and dry cake mix.
- Place one-third of the dry mixture on the bottom of the slow cooker.
- Place half of the can of pie filling over the dry ingredients.
- Repeat the layers until all the ingredients are used, ending with the dry mix.
- Cover and cook on high for 1½ hours or on low for 3½ to 4 hours.
- Serve from the slow cooker. *Do not invert this dessert.* (For information on spoon cakes and spoon desserts please read page 193.)

Yield: 12 (3-ounce) servings

Calories: 249; Fat: 4g (16% fat); Cholesterol: 0mg; Carbohydrate: 50g; Dietary Fiber: 2g; Protein: 3g; Sodium: 283mg

Cherry Cobbler Spoon Dessert

Oh, man, this is so-o-o good. It's hard to eat only one serving.

1 (18.25-ounce) box cherry chip-flavored cake mix, dry (I use Betty Crocker Super Moist.) Do not make as directed on box.	1 (20-ounce) can light cherry pie filling

- Spray a slow cooker with nonfat cooking spray.
- Spread half of the cake mix in the bottom of the slow cooker.
- Spread half the can of pie filling over the dry cake mix.
- Repeat the layers.
- Cover and cook on high for 2 hours.
- Remove the servings from the slow cooker. *Do not invert this dessert.* Serve directly from the slow cooker. (For information on spoon cakes and spoon desserts please read page 193.)

Yield: 12 (3-ounce) servings

Calories: 203; Fat: 5g (23% fat); Cholesterol: 11mg; Carbohydrate: 36g; Dietary Fiber: 1g; Protein: 3g; Sodium: 343mg

Cherry Spoon Cake

This cake is best not frosted, but served as is, or with whipped topping.

I (18.25-ounce) box yellow cake mix	I (20-ounce) can cherry pie filling

- Preheat a slow cooker to high.
- Spray the cooker with nonfat cooking spray.
- In a medium-size bowl stir together the cake mix and pie filling until well mixed. The dough will be thick.
- Pour the dough into the slow cooker.
- Place a paper towel over the cooker. Put the lid of the cooker on top of the paper towel to cover.
- Cook on high for 2 hours or until a toothpick inserted in the middle comes out clean.
- Serve from the slow cooker. *Do not invert this dessert.* (For information on spoon cakes and spoon desserts please read page 193.)

Yield: 12 servings

Calories: 233; Fat: 4g (14% fat); Cholesterol: 0mg; Carbohydrate: 48g; Dietary
Fiber: 0g; Protein: 2g; Sodium: 298mg

Chocolate Cherry Delight
Spoon Dessert

Yummy topped with frozen vanilla yogurt. This cake is not intended to be frosted.

I	(2I-ounce) can light cherry pie filling		Super Moist with pudding in the mix.)
I	(18.25-ounce) box chocolate cake mix (I use Betty Crocker	I	teaspoon almond extract

- Preheat a slow cooker on high for 10 minutes.
- Spray the cooker with nonfat cooking spray.
- In a medium-size mixing bowl mix together the pie filling, cake mix, and almond extract. Stir for 2 minutes. The batter will be thick and lumpy.
- Pour the batter into the prepared cooker. *Do not put the lid on tightly.* Leave a ¼- to ½-inch crack between the lid and the slow cooker to allow the steam to escape.
- Cook on high for 2 hours or until a toothpick inserted in the middle comes out clean.
- Place a large serving plate with an edge (so the sauce won't overflow off the plate) upside down on top of the slow cooker. Holding the slow cooker and plate firmly together, carefully flip the cake upside down. It will be steamy hot so be *very* careful. The berries will ooze down the sides of the cake.

Note: You may want to serve this dessert with a spoon from the slow cooker if you are concerned about inverting the cake.

Yield: 12 (½-cup) servings

Calories: 203; Fat: 4g (18% fat); Cholesterol: 0mg; Carbohydrate: 40g; Dietary Fiber: 2g; Protein: 2g; Sodium: 277mg

Fruit Cocktail Spoon Cake

Tasty with fudge drizzled over top.

I (13.3-ounce) Betty Crocker's Super Moist Creamy Swirls yellow cake mix, dry	I (15-ounce) can light fruit cocktail

- Preheat a cooker on high while preparing the cake.
- Spray the slow cooker with nonfat cooking spray.
- Set aside the packet of fudge from the box of the cake mix.
- In a medium-size bowl stir together the dry cake mix (without the fudge) and the fruit cocktail with the juice. Stir until thick, creamy, and lumpy.
- Pour the mixture into the prepared slow cooker.
- Put the lid on the slow cooker, leaving a $\frac{1}{4}$- to $\frac{1}{2}$-inch opening to allow moisture to escape.
- Cook on high for 2 hours.
- Spoon the servings from the slow cooker. *Do not invert this dessert.* If desired drizzle the fudge from the packet in the cake mix box over each serving.

Yield: 9 ($\frac{1}{2}$-cup) servings

Calories: 200; Fat: 4g (18% fat); Cholesterol: 0mg; Carbohydrate: 39g; Dietary Fiber: 1g; Protein: 2g; Sodium: 251mg

Spiced Fruity Spoon Cake

Very moist and tasty.

1 **(16-ounce) can light fruit cocktail**	1 **teaspoon cinnamon**
2 **egg whites**	¹/₃ **cup flour**
1 **(18.25-ounce) box yellow cake mix**	

- Preheat a slow cooker to high.
- Spray the cooker with nonfat cooking spray.
- In a medium-size mixing bowl stir together the fruit cocktail with the juice, egg whites, cake mix, cinnamon, and flour until well mixed. The dough will be thick.
- Pour the mixture into the prepared slow cooker.
- Place a paper towel over the cooker. Put the lid of the cooker on top of the paper towel to cover.
- Cook on high for 2 hours or until a toothpick inserted in the center comes out clean.
- Serve from the slow cooker. *Do not invert this dessert.* (For information on spoon cakes and spoon desserts please read page 193.)

Yield: 12 (3-ounce) servings

Calories: 216; Fat: 4g (15% fat); Cholesterol: 0mg; Carbohydrate: 44g; Dietary Fiber: 1g; Protein: 3g; Sodium: 301mg

Hot Fudge Spoon Cake

Super moist. Super delicious. I like to whip this up quickly before church. When I get home from church, it's an extra special treat everyone loves to devour. Many say it is their favorite of my desserts.

3	cups skim milk	1¹/₃	cups water
1	(5-ounce) box chocolate cook and serve pudding mix (I use Jell-O.)	¹/₂	cup applesauce
1	(18.25-ounce) Betty Crocker's Super Moist Chocolate Fudge cake mix, dry	6	egg whites

- Spray a slow cooker with nonfat cooking spray.
- With a whisk mix the skim milk with the chocolate pudding in the cooker until completely dissolved.
- In a medium-size bowl with a whisk mix the dry cake mix, water, applesauce, and egg whites together for 2 minutes or until well-blended.
- Gently pour the cake batter into the middle of the *not*-cooked pudding mixture in the slow cooker.
- Cover and cook on high for 2¹/₂ hours.
- Serve hot with a fat-free ice cream. *Do not invert this dessert.* Spoon the servings from the slow cooker. (For information on spoon cakes and spoon desserts please read page 193.)

Note: If desired, after 2¹/₂ hours of cooking, unplug the slow cooker. The dessert will stay warm and delicious for hours. It travels well to potlucks or social gatherings.

Note: The cake will firm as if it were baked, yet the pudding will still be thick and creamy. When serving make sure you reach to the bottom of your slow cooker to get the creamy pudding with each serving of cake.

Yield: 15 servings

Calories: 206; Fat: 3g (14% fat); Cholesterol: 1mg; Carbohydrate: 40g; Dietary Fiber: 1g; Protein: 5g; Sodium: 305mg

Lemon Spoon Cake
with Lemon Sauce

Terrific!

1 (4½-ounce) box lemon-flavored, cook-and-serve pudding—Do not make as directed on the box.	3 egg whites
2½ plus 1¼ cups water	1 (18.25-ounce) box white cake mix (I use Betty Crocker Super Moist.) Do not make as directed on box.
¾ cup sugar or no-calorie sweetener (I use Splenda, the kind that measures like sugar, not the individual packets.)	1 (3-ounce) box lemon-flavored gelatin (I use Jell-O.) Do not make as directed on box.
	⅓ cup applesauce

- Preheat a slow cooker to high.
- Spray the slow cooker with nonfat cooking spray.
- Stir the pudding mix, the 2½ cups water, and sugar together in the slow cooker until completely dissolved.
- In a large bowl beat the egg whites for 2 minutes or until foamy.
- Stir into the foamy egg whites the cake mix, gelatin, applesauce, and the remaining 1¼ cups of water. Gently stir for 2 minutes. The batter will be lumpy.
- Pour the cake batter into the pudding mixture in the slow cooker. Do not stir.
- Place a paper towel on top of the slow cooker. Cover by placing the lid of the slow cooker on the paper towel.
- Cook on high for 2 hours.
- Remove the lid and paper towel.
- Unplug the slow cooker, and if possible, remove the crock from the slow cooker. Let it sit for 10 minutes.
- Serve this dessert from the slow cooker. *Do not turn upside down.* (For information on spoon cakes and spoon desserts please read page 193.)

Yield: 12 servings

(Made with sugar): Calories: 316; Fat: 5g (15% fat); Cholesterol: 53mg; Carbohydrate: 63g; Dietary Fiber: 1g; Protein: 4g; Sodium: 367mg
(Made with Splenda): Calories: 268; Fat: 5g (16% fat); Cholesterol: 53mg; Carbohydrate: 59g; Dietary Fiber: 1g; Protein: 4g; Sodium: 367mg

Peaches & Cream Spoon Cake

Super moist and super delicious.

1 (15$^1/_4$-ounce) can peaches in light syrup	1 (18.25-ounce) classic white cake mix, dry (I use Duncan Hines.)
$^1/_2$ teaspoon ground allspice	$^1/_2$ cup quick-cooking oats
$^1/_2$ plus $^1/_4$ teaspoon ground cinnamon, plus additional for topping, optional	24 tablespoons fat-free whipped topping

- Preheat a slow cooker on high.
- Spray the slow cooker with nonfat cooking spray.
- In a blender purée the peaches with the peach syrup, allspice, and the $^1/_2$ teaspoon cinnamon until smooth and no peaches are visible.
- Pour the puréed peaches into the cooker.
- Set aside $^1/_2$ cup dry cake mix for later.
- Pour the remaining box of dry cake mix into the slow cooker with the puréed peaches.
- Stir for 2 minutes. (There still may be lumps in the batter.)
- In a bowl stir together the dry oatmeal and the reserved $^1/_2$ cup of the dry cake mix until well mixed.
- Gently sprinkle the mixture on top of the batter in the slow cooker.
- Sprinkle the remaining $^1/_4$ teaspoon cinnamon on top.
- Place a paper towel over the slow cooker.
- Put the lid of the slow cooker on the paper towel to cover.
- Cook on high for 2 hours.
- Spoon the cake out while still warm or hot onto each serving dish. *Do not invert.* (For information on spoon cakes and spoon desserts please read page 193.)
- Top each serving with 2 tablespoons whipped topping.
- If desired, sprinkle with cinnamon.

Note: Refrigerate unused portions. The cake is also good chilled.

Yield: 12 ($^1/_2$-cup) servings

Calories: 225; Fat: 5g (18% fat); Cholesterol: 3mg; Carbohydrate: 44g; Dietary Fiber: 1g; Protein: 3g; Sodium: 286mg

Pineapple Cobbler Spoon Dessert

Very rich.

I (18.25-ounce) yellow cake mix, dry (I use Betty Crocker Super Moist.) Do not make as directed.	Fat-free whipped topping, optional
I (20-ounce) can crushed pineapple in pineapple juice, not drained	

- Spray a slow cooker with nonfat cooking spray.
- Set ⅓ cup of the dry cake mix aside.
- Sprinkle half of the remaining dry cake mix in the bottom of the slow cooker.
- Spread half of the can of the crushed pineapple over the dry cake mix.
- Repeat the layers until the ingredients are used up.
- Sprinkle the ⅓ cup dry cake mix that was previously set aside on top of the crushed pineapple.
- Cover and cook on high for 2 hours.
- Serve hot with a dab of whipped topping, optional. *Do not invert this dessert.* Serve from the slow cooker. (For information on spoon cakes and spoon desserts please read page 193.)

Yield: 12 (3-ounce) servings

Calories: 205; Fat: 3g (15% fat); Cholesterol: 0mg; Carbohydrate: 42g; Dietary Fiber: 0g; Protein: 2g; Sodium: 294mg

Warm Cherry Trifle Spoon Dessert

Tastes as good as it looks.

1 cup powdered sugar	1/4 cup chopped pecans or walnuts
1 (8-ounce) package fat-free cream cheese, at room temperature	5 cups cubed angel food cake
	1 (20-ounce) can light cherry pie filling
1 (8-ounce) container fat-free whipped topping	

- Beat together the powdered sugar and fat-free cream cheese. Add the whipped topping and chopped nuts. Stir in the angel food cake cubes.
- Pour half the cake mixture into the cooker.
- Pour half of the can of cherry pie filling on top of the cake mix.
- Repeat the layers until all the ingredients have been used.
- Cook on low for 1 hour.
- Serve from the slow cooker. *Do not invert this dessert.* (For information on spoon cakes and spoon desserts please read page 193.)

Yield: 15 (½-cup) servings

Calories: 148; Fat: 2g (10% fat); Cholesterol: 1mg; Carbohydrate: 29g; Dietary Fiber: 1g; Protein: 3g; Sodium: 227mg

★ **Blueberry Trifle:** Substitute 1 can light blueberry pie filling in place of the cherry pie filling.

Yield: 15 (½-cup) servings

Calories: 148; Fat: 2g (10% fat); Cholesterol: 1mg; Carbohydrate: 29g; Dietary Fiber: 1g; Protein: 3g; Sodium: 227mg

Zucchini Spoon Cake

A delicious treat.

1¹/₂ teaspoons ground cinnamon	¹/₂ cup applesauce
6 egg whites	3 cups finely shredded zucchini
1 (18.25-ounce) yellow cake mix, dry (I use Betty Crocker Super Moist.)	¹/₂ cup raisins
	¹/₄ cup chopped walnuts

- Preheat a slow cooker on high for 10 minutes.
- Spray the cooker with nonfat cooking spray.
- With a mixer beat together the cinnamon, egg whites, cake mix, and applesauce for 2 minutes.
- With a spatula gently stir in the zucchini, raisins, and walnuts.
- Pour the mixture into the prepared cooker.
- Cover and cook on high for 1³/₄ hours or until a toothpick inserted in the center comes out clean.

Yield: 15 servings

Calories: 187; Fat: 4g (20% fat); Cholesterol: 0mg; Carbohydrate: 35g; Dietary Fiber: 1g; Protein: 4g; Sodium: 255mg

Index

About Solid Rock

A portion of my books' profits go to help support the noteworthy and honorable efforts of an inner-city children and teens outreach program called Solid Rock in Toledo, Ohio. With hands-on involvement Pastor Keith Stepp and his wonderful wife, Shannon, along with their growing support staff, focus on the needs of the central city, crossing over racial and economic barriers.

Through their children and teens' programs they are establishing a moral foundation for our future generations based on biblical principles. We are in constant need of volunteers to help in many areas, including child sponsors. To be a child sponsor, simply contact Solid Rock and let them know you would like to sponsor a child:

Solid Rock Outreach Program
1630 Broadway
Toledo, Ohio 43609
Or call (419) 244-7020.

On behalf of the children and teens I thank you very much for your support of the Solid Rock Outreach Program through your purchase of my cookbooks.

Dawn

About the Author

D awn Hall is currently publishing her Busy People's line of cookbooks, including *Busy People's Slow Cooker Cookbook*.

Dawn is a successful recovering compulsive overeater and food addict. She was born watching her weight. As an accomplished aerobics instructor and facilitator for W.O.W. (Watching Our Weight), Dawn walks her talk and is living proof that you can have your cake and eat it, too.

She strongly believes her talent for creating extremely low-fat, mouth-watering foods that are made quickly and effortlessly is a gift from God.

As a popular inspirational speaker and veteran talk show guest, Dawn has appeared on *The 700 Club*, CBN, *Woman to Woman*, *Good Morning*, *A.M.*, along with numerous other TV and radio programs nationwide.

To contact Dawn or for more information on booking her for your next women's event, conference, or retreat call, write, or fax:

Dawn Hall
5425 S. Fulton-Lucas Road
Swanton, OH 43558
(419) 826-2665 or Fax (419) 826-2700
Dawn@DawnHallCookbooks.com
www.DawnHallCookbooks.com